W9-AYX-612

823.912   Ellmann, Richard,   1
JOYCE   1918-1987.
             Ulysses on the Liffey.   New York,
           Oxford University, c1972.
             xviii, 208 p.   illus., facsims.   23cm.
           index
                EUREKA-HUMBOLDT LIBRARY
             Facsims. on lining papers.

             Includes bibliographical references.

             1. Joyce, James, 1882-1941.   Ulysses.
           I. Title.
           PR6019.O9U64   1972

BK-8 AUG '74

FO-4 APR '74

ULYSSES ON THE LIFFEY

BY THE SAME AUTHOR

Yeats: The Man and the Masks
The Identity of Yeats
(Faber and Faber)

James Joyce
Eminent Domain: Yeats among Wilde, Joyce, Pound,
Eliot, and Auden
(Oxford University Press)

translation
Selected Writings of Henri Michaux
(Routledge and Kegan Paul)

edited works
Stanislaus Joyce: My Brother's Keeper
The Critical Writings of James Joyce
(with Ellsworth Mason)
Letters of James Joyce (Volumes II and III)
James Joyce: Giacomo Joyce
(Faber and Faber)

Arthur Symons: The Symbolist Movement in Literature
(E. P. Dutton & Co)
Edwardians and Late Victorians
(Columbia University Press)
The Modern Tradition (with Charles Feidelson, Jr)
(Oxford University Press)
The Artist as Critic: Critical Writings of Oscar Wilde
(W. H. Allen)
Oscar Wilde: Twentieth Century Views
(Prentice-Hall Inc.)

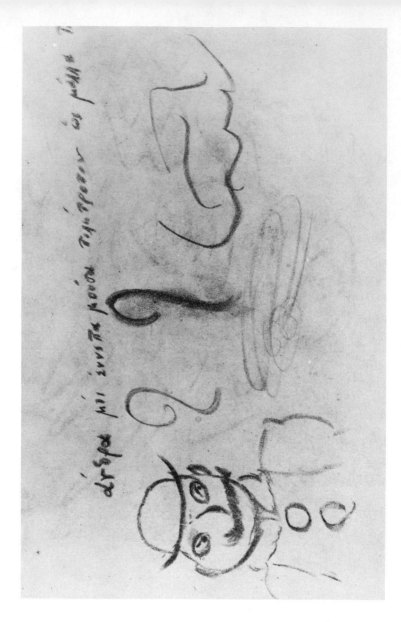

A 'portrait' of Leopold Bloom by James Joyce, drawn in Myron C. Nutting's Paris studio in 1923 [?]. The Greek line is the beginning of the *Odyssey*, 'Tell me, Muse, of the man of many devices, who over many ways . . .'

Ulysses on the Liffey

Richard Ellmann

New York
Oxford University Press
1972

EUREKA-HUMBOLDT LIBRARY

©Copyright Richard Ellmann 1972

Library of Congress Catalogue Card Number: 79-190477

The quotations from *Ulysses* are with
the kind permission of
Random House, Inc.

Printed in the United States of America

*Thinking
about
Mary*

CONTENTS

* The number in brackets refers to the relevant episode in *Ulysses*.

ILLUSTRATIONS

PREFACE

After fifty years *Ulysses* still presents itself as the most difficult of entertaining novels, and the most entertaining of difficult ones. To read it is not enough, one must read it with unwonted attention, and read it again. Even then it keeps some of its mysteries. Joyce's purposes in the book are not nearly so public as might be expected from his having helped Stuart Gilbert to write a book-long commentary on it, or from his having supplied Frank Budgen with much material on its composition. To divulge his means was one thing, his meaning another.

That he should have written *Ulysses* as a comedy went back to a decision of early youth. He had made some effort to write tragedy in the manner of Ibsen, but concluded that comedy was his true mode. He liked comedy both in its larger sense of negotiating the reconciliation of forces, and in its more immediate sense of provoking laughter. Sympathy and incongruity were his gregarious substitutes for pity and terror. To Joyce tragedy centred in privation, comedy in possession; tragedy in lamentation, comedy in joy; tragedy in élitism, comedy in democracy. The comic method might take varied forms, malapropism or epigram, rolypoly farce or distant satire, parody or mock-heroics. But all its means must coalesce in a view which, in early life at least, Joyce was willing to call his faith.

About this faith he wrote to Lady Gregory at the age of twenty, 'though I seem to have been driven out of my country here as a misbeliever I have found no man yet with a faith like mine'. It was not a subject on which, being a reticent man, he was likely to dilate; but in a letter of 1912, as well as in the ending of *A Portrait of the Artist as a Young Man*, Joyce spoke of himself as one of those trying to instil a soul or conscience into his 'wretched race'. The faith was not Christian, or in any way institutional, but it had its own rigorousness. In some manner his books were conceived as creating and measuring social value.

Different as they are in merit, *Ulysses* and *A Portrait* are to this extent companion pieces. The early book was achieved by narrowing in upon the experiences described in *Stephen Hero*, to the exclusion of what was not immediately relevant; the later book was more copious in intent, determined to afford a place to all that Joyce had cut out from *A Portrait* and much more, to make irrelevance relevant to a larger plan. *Ulysses* was in fact designed to be related to other large works, encyclopedias and dictionaries. It is lexical in its regard for English, as it takes in words from all periods, social levels, expressive stances. As its title suggests, it makes the major works of western culture, beginning with the *Odyssey*, tributary to it as it is tributary to them; it also marks the outlines of western history and philosophy. But most of all, Joyce was bent upon creating a comedy which, without being divine like Dante's — he thought divinity alien to him — would have the complexity of a medieval myth.

A recent writer on Joyce has said that after fifty years there is no point in looking for a new myth for *Ulysses*, but it is just that which I propose. Needless to say, Joyce's myth has four aspects — all good myths have. The first is literal: this is the narrative of Stephen's estrangement from Mulligan, Molly Bloom's infidelity, the meeting of Bloom and Stephen, their return to the Blooms' house and eventual parting. The thread is thin but sufficient for a new odyssey in which most of the adventures occur inside the mind. The second aspect is ethical, involving certain discriminations between desirable and undesirable life. The third is aesthetic, and presents a relationship between art and nature, as between art and morality. The last is anagogic, the ultimate justification of existence. The book concludes with an absorption of the first three levels into the fourth. To unite this lofty purpose with the most ordinary circumstances Joyce engaged the extravagances of comedy.

He began less than two years after he left Dublin in his self-imposed and self-titled exile. In September 1906 he wrote to his brother from Rome that he would add to *Dubliners* a new story, 'Ulysses', about a man named Hunter. Six weeks later he still planned to do it, but had 'too many cares at present'. Then in February 1907 he announced that 'Ulysses' 'never got any forrader than the title', although it could still be written 'if circumstances were favourable'. They did not become so for seven years, but in that Biblical span bits and pieces of his life in Dublin, modified by his absence from Dublin in Trieste, were slowly magnetized.

The actual composition of *Ulysses* began in 1914, a bumper year, for Joyce at any rate, in which he also drafted his play *Exiles*, published *Dubliners*, wrote his prose poem *Giacomo Joyce*, and completed the last two chapters of *A Portrait of the Artist*. He ended this book with events which in his life had occurred at the beginning of December 1902, though he re-dated them to flowery spring rather than to barren winter. His two Paris sojourns, and the months from his return to Dublin in April 1903 until his departure in October 1904, converge into *Ulysses*. This period appeared aimless to others, but it had the virtue of incubating his decision to leave Ireland for good. Looking backward at these months, he could see three incidents, above all, as generative clusters, integral in his development and in his plans for his fiction.

The first of these in time was his meeting with Nora Barnacle on a Dublin street. They agreed to meet again, but she failed to show up. A letter of Joyce, written on 15 June, regrets her failure and asks her to name another night. That they first walked out together on 16 June is reasonably certain. In later life Mrs Joyce referred to 16 June as the day that she and her husband had first *met*; she knew the date of *Ulysses* had been chosen in relation to her, but either forgot or preferred to veil that it pertained to a more momentous interview than their first. While Joyce incorporated some aspects of his wife into Molly Bloom, and granted both her and her husband a tender memory of a day in their courtship, he did not otherwise imitate in his book this rendezvous. Yet he centred 'Bloomsday' on that date.

Two subsequent events of the same period receive in *Ulysses* more direct mention. The book's opening draws upon Joyce's quarrel with Oliver St John Gogarty. He and Joyce had been faint friends for over a year, and Gogarty had formed a plan of living with Joyce in the Martello tower at Sandycove. This tower was one of seventy-four which the British had hastily flung up along the English and Irish coasts in 1804 to forestall a French invasion. Unlike most of the others, it had only recently been evacuated by the army. It was to be a symbolic dwelling. In a notebook he kept in Trieste, Joyce noted under Gogarty's name that 'The Omphalos' (Gogarty called the tower the *Omphalos* or navelstone like that of Delphi) 'was to be the temple of a neo-paganism'; and in Joyce's play *Exiles* the hero remembers an equivalent habitation which aspired to be 'the hearth of a new life'.

Gogarty leased the tower in August, but by that time

Joyce's relations with him were strained by a broadside, 'The Holy Office', in which Joyce ridiculed most of the writers in Dublin, and did not exempt Gogarty. Nevertheless, when Joyce had no other place to go and no money, he presented himself at the tower on 9 September. He was allowed in, as his brother noted in a diary, 'on sufferance'.

Another guest in the tower was Samuel Chenevix Trench, a principal model for the character Haines in *Ulysses*. On the night of 14 September, Trench had a nightmare of a black panther, and began to shoot at it with a gun. Gogarty got the gun away and added a barrage of his own, aimed at the pots and pans above Joyce's bed. Upon this notice of eviction, Joyce dressed and left. The incident ended the friendship, but he drew a larger significance from it: he determined to have done with all Ireland. That night, while waiting for Nora Barnacle, he thought (as he wrote her next day) 'that I was fighting a battle with every religious and social force in Ireland for you and that I had nothing to rely on but myself'. In this mood he asked her if she could 'choose to stand beside me' and go abroad. She agreed without hesitation.

Ten years later Joyce perceived how this débâcle with Gogarty might, suitably adapted, provide his book with a first scene. He had also another incident which could serve as the climax of his book. On the night of 22 June 1904 Joyce (not as yet committed either to Nora Barnacle or to monogamy) got himself into a brawl, probably involving a girl on the street. After a skirmish he was left with 'black eye, sprained wrist, sprained ankle, cut chin, cut hand'. Next day he lamented to a friend, 'For one role at least I seem unfit – that of man of honour.' He did not mention what in retrospect evidently became the most impressive aspect of the fracas; it was probably on this occasion that he was dusted off

and taken home by a man named Alfred Hunter. This was the
Hunter about whom the short story 'Ulysses' was to be projected. Presumably that story would have shown Hunter
circumnavigating Dublin, and in the end offering a lifebuoy
to a castaway resembling Joyce.

Hunter was rumoured to be Jewish and to have an unfaithful wife, two disparate points that became important
later. Joyce did not know him well, having (according to
Stanislaus Joyce) met him only once or twice. This very lack
of acquaintance added to the interest of the occasion, since
Joyce regarded himself as hemmed in by indifference or hostility, and was the more surprised that someone unfamiliar, of
temperament and background seemingly opposite, should
have causelessly defended him. Here might be one of those
'epiphanies' – sudden, unlooked-for turns in experience –
which could prove the more momentous for being modest.

The book that emerged as *Ulysses* was grounded in these
events but not limited by their contours. Joyce wrote his
book out of fact, and also out of fire. Some of the fire went
into his passion for form. The book's total meaning depends
so heavily upon a perception of its form that any hints by the
author demand attention. At first, Joyce chose to insist upon
his book's Odyssean parallels, but after inserting them into
the serial publication of some chapters, he removed them,
evidently confident that the book might be taken on its own
terms. Yet he was not comfortable at the thought that his art
might too successfully conceal his art, and made sure that
Stuart Gilbert revived the Homeric titles for his book, *James
Joyce's 'Ulysses'*, in 1934.

The famous table of colours, techniques, organs, and other
aspects of *Ulysses*, which Gilbert printed in his book, had a
predecessor in one which Joyce made for Carlo Linati in

September 1920. In the letter accompanying it he remarked, 'My intention is not only to render the myth *sub specie temporis nostri* but also to allow each adventure (that is, every hour, every organ, every art being interconnected and interrelated in the structural scheme of the whole) to condition and even to create its own technique. Each adventure is so to speak one person although it is composed of persons – as Aquinas relates of the heavenly hosts.'

In the Appendix to this book the two schemas, one sent to Linati, the other to Gilbert, are compared. Neither schema exhibits the interrelationships in the way that Joyce evidently had in mind, so the total plan has to be put together largely from internal evidence, and this is what I have attempted to do here. The design proves to be much more elaborate than Joyce ever formally indicated, yet beautifully simple in its purport. It has, as Joyce indicated to Wyndham Lewis one day when they were walking near Notre Dame, something of the complexity sought by the makers of cathedrals. In writing a new *Odyssey* Joyce superimposed elements of the medieval upon elements of the classical mind. But both are drawn into modern experience so that they have a present rather than an atavistic life.

The interpretation of *Ulysses* in the pages that follow was largely developed in the course of preparing the T. S. Eliot Memorial Lectures, which I had the honour of delivering at the University of Kent in Canterbury in May 1971. I am indebted to the University of Kent for their invitation, and to Professor F. S. L. Lyons for his hospitable sponsorship. Peter du Sautoy of Faber and Faber was most considerate in his arrangements for this book.

Mary Ellmann, to whom this book is gratefully dedicated,

observed its early stages with amusement, but then made me aware of many additional possibilities. I have also learned from Mary Reynolds, whose own important work on Dante and Joyce will soon be published. Catharine Carver allowed me to benefit from her subtle and exacting criticism and her constant encouragement. Ottocaro Weiss, shortly before his death, took much trouble to help me with Joyce's Italian schema for *Ulysses*. I have profited from conversations with Robert O'Clair, Peter Gay, Charles Feidelson, and J. B. Hainsworth. I am indebted to my friends David Du Vivier and S. Schoenbaum for help in securing some of the illustrations. I wish to thank the Guggenheim Foundation for generous assistance.

New College, Oxford   R. E.
20 June 1971

ULYSSES ON THE LIFFEY

Homer Contemplates Aristotle

While in Trieste Joyce remarked of his book *Dubliners* that he took little satisfaction in it because it rewarded him with no sense of having overcome difficulties in the writing. When in 1914 he started *Ulysses*, he did not intend to be short on difficulties again. For perhaps a year his plan was kept fluid, on a principle he enunciated later, that it was best not to plan everything in advance, so that good things would be free to emerge in the course of composition. Accordingly, the number of episodes was still unfixed in June 1915, by which time he was well along with the opening chapters. He sent a post-card to his brother Stanislaus, then interned as a prisoner-of-war by the Austrians, in which he announced that the first part of his book would have four episodes, the second part fifteen, and the third part three. It is speculative but likely that the total of twenty-two episodes was based upon Stephen's age, which was also his own, twenty-two, in 1904 when the book was supposed to take place. (Homer had used twenty-four books, divided into three parts of four, eight, and twelve books.) But if this was Joyce's notion, he relinquished it. Only the third part remained, unchangeably, in three episodes; the second shrank from fifteen to twelve; and the first part from four to three.

The result of these modifications was to make the book move in groups of three, with the beginning and ending (*Telemachiad* and *Return*) a little separated from the twelve adventures (in four triads) of the middle. The number three proved to be for Joyce, as it was for Dante, the determining element of structure. It was Homer's favourite number as well. Having adopted the triadic organization, Joyce planned that each triad should embody thesis, antithesis, and synthesis. One symmetry required another: if one chapter is external, the next is internal, and the third a mixture; similarly, if one episode centres on land, the second will be watery, and the third amphibious; if one is solar, the second will be lunar, and the third will envisage an alchemical marriage of sun and moon; if the first is body, the second is soul, the third is their tentative unity. These will be seen to be the lineaments of Joyce's creation.

Because of the complicated interlinking of episodes, Joyce had to lace early and late chapters with anticipations or reverberations of other chapters. This process continued into 1922 through the many sets of proofs that the printer and publisher allowed him, so that the book could only reach completion all together, each of its parts echoing all the others simultaneously.

Throughout his work, Joyce remained loyal to what was patently his object in entitling the book *Ulysses* – to blend the two ends of the western tradition like a multitemporal, multiterritorial pun. Stephen Dedalus, in a prideful moment of *A Portrait of the Artist as a Young Man*, feels that all ages are as one to him, and some such melting of time, and of space, Joyce was now determined to bring about. He had therefore to give new Ireland an old Greek inflection, to fulfil what Mulligan throws out to Stephen, 'If you and I could only work together we might do something for the island. Hellenise it.' Stephen Dedalus already has a Greek name, which Mulligan finds absurd. Mulligan is himself fond of quoting Homer in Greek, he describes the tower as the *omphalos*, and his gold teeth remind Stephen of a saint with a Greek name, Chrysostomos.

Why then did Joyce not make his Ulysses a modern Greek? For someone who relied heavily on familiar materials, the fact that he did not have a modern Greek at hand was a deterrent. But even if he had had one, the parallel was to be sought elsewhere than in racial continuity. He was not planning to follow Homer so ethnically. In Stephen Dedalus he had invented a Greek-Irishman, in Bloom he could invent another, who would also be 'a jewgreek'. The comparison of the Irish to the Israelites was a familiar one in Irish rhetoric, and even Gladstone compared Parnell to Moses. For adding a Greek component Joyce might have claimed that the Jews, probably unlike modern Greeks, can trace themselves back to Homeric times. He was more interested in a theory he encountered in Victor Bérard's *Les Phéniciens et l'Odyssée* (1902), that the *Odyssey* had Semitic origins. It was a scholarly confirmation for what he had already determined to do.

Joyce could have made his Jewish hero orthodox, an archaic survivor from a past older than Homer into an unfamiliar and gentile world. But while the antiquity of the Jews undoubtedly attracted Joyce, he had no real interest in Judaism as a religion, and gave Bloom none. The models he probably had in mind for his hero were conspicuously remote from religious zeal: Alfred Hunter was scarcely Jewish, and Ettore Schmitz (Italo Svevo) had married a Christian. Because of Joyce's liking for fact, the history of these *Ur*-Blooms is not irrelevant. When asked why Bloom was the son of a Hungarian, Joyce replied, 'Because he was.' (Svevo's grandfather was Hungarian.) Bloom must register, with Jewish characteristics, the same impress of Christianity that, as Stephen indicates (and as Joyce had noted in his alphabetical notebook), everyone now must, so he gave Bloom a history of easyminded conversion to Protestantism and Catholicism, and of course situated him in a Catholic country. In this way he pillowed the Judaeo-Christian tradition upon the Hebrew-Hellenic one. But Bloom had also to be a twentieth-century man, and Joyce therefore conferred upon him the grace of unbelief. As a freethinker Bloom is post-Christian, just as, being a Christian convert, he is post-Judaic, and being Judaic-Christian he is post-Homeric. Joyce's book comprehends layer upon layer of the past.

The role of Stephen Dedalus stirred an odd problem. If we try to imagine Joyce's vexations in getting started, one must have been that, as he remarked to Frank Budgen, Stephen had a shape that couldn't be changed. It was a shape left over from *A Portrait of the Artist as a Young Man*. In that book much of the imagery had derived from the name of Dedalus and its association with the legendary maker of mazes and wings. Now it was incumbent upon Stephen to shift suddenly from one Greek myth to another, to become Odysseus' son. Myth-hopping is not easy. Joyce solved the problem with admirable boldness. Instead of dropping the Daedalean connection, he emphasized it. Stephen is unique in literature in that he is the son of two fathers, Odysseus and Dedalus. After Mulligan's mockery of the name Dedalus, Stephen berates himself, because of the failure of his Paris junket, as a foolhardy Icarus, an errant son rather than an independent inventor, a sea-bedabbled lapwing. In this way the name stretches a little, and the reminder that Daedalus and Icarus were father and son prepares for more metaphors about fatherhood and sonhood. Joyce could find support in an extraordinary speech of Telemachus in the first book of the *Odyssey*: asked by Athena if he is really Odysseus' son, he responds, 'My mother says I am

4

his son, but I don't know myself; I never heard of anyone who did know whose son he was.' Bloom and Stephen were not and could not be related by blood, but they might be related – as fathers and sons so often are not – by temperament, by comparable feelings, lacks, needs.

That Bloom should feel paternal towards Stephen was easier than for Stephen to feel filial towards Bloom. Joyce could easily make Bloom's son Rudy die eleven days after birth, but he could not very well kill off Simon Dedalus without diverging more than he liked from the actual pattern of events. Telemachus is not Oedipus, is rather the opposite of Oedipus. Two dead parents for Stephen would on all counts be excessive. But if the relationship was metaphorical and not actual, then Stephen could simply have mislaid his father in the pub and could long for an image of fatherhood more comprehensive than his, or perhaps any, biological parent could provide. Joyce felt an incongruity between his genetic origins in a shiftless father and an orthodox mother, fond of them though he was, and his imaginative origins in Ibsen, Flaubert, Dante, and D'Annunzio. Without abjuring their actual parents, he and Stephen doted on the mystery of multiple parentage. Behind Joyce's characters lie other created characters, behind his creative acts other creators throng, lending a hand when they can. They concede continuity, they confirm the centrality of Joyce's undertaking. They constitute an invisible but companionable congeries of presences, an ancestry.

The incongruity which Joyce now developed was that between a self-willed young man and an assimilative older one, between youth and middle age. If the two men were at once alike and different, he might orient them so they would draw closer and closer together. The risk would be that the relation might seem sentimental, or perhaps, homosexual. But they need not draw so close as that; the main thing was that they should complete each other, as the treble the bass. Friday completes Robinson Crusoe by challenging with naïveté Crusoe's technological complacency, and Sancho Panza completes Don Quixote by shrewdly undermining his right to make his own world. In a way, Joyce attempted something more difficult still, because the relation of his two characters had to be mostly furtive rather than open, and because he did not allow either to be master.

Beginning the book in 1914, Joyce was able to make use of certain material left over from *A Portrait of the Artist*. (His method of starting *Finnegans Wake* was also to sort out notes unused for *Ulysses*.) The surviving manuscript pages of *A Portrait* have to do with a plan by Stephen and a young man named Goggins – who is intermediate between Gogarty and Mulligan – to occupy a tower. They indicate that at one time Joyce may have thought of bringing *A Portrait* on through his second departure from Dublin, a more companionable one than the first, though less grand, in that he had a girl on his arm. He gave up the idea, perhaps because, under the influence of his excitement over *Ulysses*, he saw that the first novel could best end in the wilful isolation of the hero so that the second might end in a renewal of relationships. In a sense his own elopement with Nora Barnacle symbolized exactly that. By leaving out of the first book his two sojourns in Paris, of late 1902 and early 1903, and the months before and after his mother's death on 13 August 1903, during which he moved about Dublin feeling talented and trammelled, Joyce had sufficient unused grumpiness to thicken Stephen's consciousness in the opening chapters of *Ulysses*. *A Portrait* had begun with dense memories, there inspired by fever as here by grief; Stephen's consciousness is here atomized rather than whorled as there.

In *Ulysses* Stephen is still, after almost a year, in mourning for his mother. The fact that he is bereaved connects him with the bereaved Hamlet, who however had lost a different parent. Joyce is here far from Homer, where Ulysses, not Telemachus, has lost a mother, and where Telemachus' concern is for a father who is lost and not dead. But by now this identity-glide between father and son had become part of Joyce's method. Variations brought new meanings and destroyed old ones. He claimed authority over prototypes as over quotations.

One connection, Shakespearean as well as Homeric, that Joyce resolved to keep, was the theme of usurpation. In the *Odyssey* Telemachus is aroused to search for his father in part because his mother's suitors are devouring his food and consuming his property. In *Hamlet* the prince complains about his mother's successful suitor. But Stephen's mother is dead, and when alive she had no suitors. Joyce may have considered continuing that rivalry of Stephen and Cranly for the same girl which was shadowed in the concluding pages of *A Portrait*. He obviously considered also the possibility of making all the events occur later, of giving Stephen a girl, and of having him in danger of being cuckolded by a friend. But instead he moved this material into a separate work, his play *Exiles*, where the hero, by now a father himself, returns to Ithacan Dublin and eggs on a suitor for his wife only to put him to rout. (He also has a friend of his own named Beatrice.) So in *Ulysses*, as in the *Odyssey* but not in *Hamlet*, the sexual theme is borne exclusively by the older man. In Joyce's mind his three books, on which he was working all at once, must have represented different shoots of self-exfoliation.

For *Ulysses* Joyce devised a sketchy parallel with the *Odyssey* by beginning with the tower episode and having Stephen rather than Mulligan pay the rent. (In humble fact Gogarty paid it, not Joyce.) By this switch Mulligan, in demanding the only tower key, might be made to look a little like a usurper. If this form of usurpation sounds pretty mild, Joyce saw it would serve. He even made the word 'Usurper', which invades Stephen's mind as he leaves Mulligan, the last word in the episode. So a tenuous analogy was pressed until it became substantial.

In part because Mulligan's usurpation of the tower key was not really comparable to the encroachments of Antinöos and the other suitors upon Penelope, or to Claudius's marriage to Hamlet's mother, Joyce drew upon another author than Homer or Shakespeare to give point to the first episode. He hinted at which author it was when he wrote of the final chapter to Frank Budgen that Molly's soliloquy might be epitomized, '*Ich bin das Fleisch das stets bejaht.*' Since Molly occupies the end of the book, it would follow that someone at the start must say, with Goethe's Mephistopheles, '*Ich bin der Geist der stets verneint.*' This role was clearly apposite for Mulligan, even if he does not declare himself openly.

The Morning After (1)

It is the morning of 16 June and it might be the morning of man. The sun is 'merrying' over the sea, the mountains are 'awaking'. Young men are savouring the bitter-sweetness of their youth. They live in a tower which is the world's navel.

Every object is clearly defined as if Adam had just given it a name, or as if Aristotle had just enmattered its essence.

Yet there is a curious air of corruption about the opening scene of *Ulysses*. It is not exactly the morning of creation, it is the morning after. Adam has sinned. Stephen has returned from Baudelairean Paris, to experience the bite of conscience over his refusal to pray to his mother's god. Mulligan opens the book by mockingly celebrating mass, as if he were some false Prometheus filching fire from heaven. The tower is no navel, but a dead, disarmed relic of military power. Lucifer has fallen from heaven and could say, about middle earth: 'Why this is hell, nor am I out of it.' A British cloud covers the Greek sun.

In writing this first episode, Joyce laid out an intricate plan, like a plan of battle. He was to comment that this chapter displayed '*Il figlio spodestato alla lotta*', the dispossessed son in combat. Stephen is surrounded by thrones, dominations, powers: there is English Haines, 'the seas' ruler', with money and a guncase, but bad dreams. He represents an Imperialism that has degenerated into shooting at phantoms and into sentimental folklorism about the occupied country. He is quick to suggest that the Jews are responsible for the troubles of modern England, anti-Semitism being Joyce's touchstone for cravenheartedness. Haines is ready to persecute, as he is ready to patronize. Irish Mulligan is ready to deny, ready to betray, with false teeth of gold and a surgeon's scalpel, not to mention a razor. There is the Irish milkwoman, servant to both of them, bullied by Mulligan and Haines for her ignorance. There is Stephen's mother, clutching at him from the other world, 'to shake and bend my soul', 'to strike me down' with her maniacal religion. And there is the priest at the end, a minor character but insistent enough to claim a structural place: unlike the other men at the Forty Foot, he wears a bathing garment, and dresses discreetly in a niche – displaying sanctified prudery, the opposite of Christ's wholehearted offer of his body in the chalice.

Stephen quarrels directly or silently with all these: he is angry at Mulligan for speaking of his mother as 'beastly dead'; he makes no effort to conciliate Haines though, as Mulligan assures him, there is money to be had by doing so. He resents the old milkwoman's respect for Mulligan and Haines, and disregard of him; he is sorry for his mother's death, tormented by it, yet freed as well. Mulligan, on the other hand, butters up Haines and bullies the milkwoman. He offers to wear puce gloves and green boots, that is, to play both the British game and the Irish one. (To corroborate fiction, Gogarty became, among other things, a jester at English country houses in the late 1920s.) He not only is in complicity with Haines, though he professes scorn of him, but he is also inclined to play along with the church which he similarly mocks; he needles Stephen for not having kneeled when his mother was dying. So Mulligan looks like a prelate and acts like a snob, a servant of church and state, a timeserver, a placeseeker, and ultimately, as Stephen anticipates, 'Ireland's gay betrayer'. His insouciance is sustained by persecution of others; he keeps searching Stephen's wound about his mother, he makes heartless fun of the milkwoman, he describes with relish the hazing of a student at Oxford whom he and others threatened to 'debag'. Denial expresses itself in cruelty.

The scene is bereft of love or even liking except for Stephen's attachment to his dead mother and the quotation from Yeats's *The Countess Cathleen*, in which Aleel sings, 'And no more turn aside and brood/Upon love's bitter mystery'. To Mulligan this is a catchphrase, to Stephen a reality. Mulligan offers instead of affection a crude libertinism: to love is to stew. He is like Goethe's Mephistopheles in having no context, his whole family being an aunt. To the extent that Mulligan is the denying spirit, Joyce was faithful to the project he mentioned to his brother, of making *Ulysses* an Irish *Faust*.

Faustian Stephen refuses to serve the British empire or the Roman Catholic Church. These take on the symbolical aspect of body and soul. His conduct is marked chiefly by refusals. In the past he refused to pray for his mother, as now he refuses to swim with Mulligan. Stephen's constant refusal to do things has not endeared him to many readers, but his situation must be kept in mind: surrounded by deniers, he must deny them. ('As they deny, deny', Joyce writes in *Chamber Music*.) He can affirm only by double negatives. But beyond his refusals is a singular loyalty. Telemachus was loyal to Penelope, but Stephen wishes to be free of his own mother. His loyalty is to another woman, his muse, his 'true Penelope'. (Joyce made this clear in his schema sent to Linati.) It is to her he remains faithful rather than succumb to Haines's patronage, Mulligan's dubious hospitality, his mother's piety. Against Mulligan's scalpel he sets his steelpen. He will not allow his art to become the cracked lookingglass of a servant, as Mulligan, Haines, and his mother would all prefer. And so the first episode ends with Stephen leaving behind the imperial Haines, the prudish priest, and Mulligan, who toadies, while mocking, to both. Not to pray, and not to swim: Stephen will not accept their spiritual or physical purification. Mulligan's attempt to be clean is like his mother's ghostly demand for his soul's cleanliness. 'They wash and tub and scrub. Agenbite of inwit. Conscience. Yet here's a spot.'

The first three episodes depend heavily upon Homer and more lightly upon Goethe and Shakespeare. Another writer – explicitly named – makes his presence felt. Rembrandt had shown the bust of Homer contemplated by Aristotle, and Joyce allows the two Greeks to contemplate each other. He had great admiration for Aristotle, and demonstrated it in many ways from 1902 to 1905. His aesthetic notebook, kept in Paris in 1903 and in Pola in 1904–5, offers extensions of Aristotle on the subjects of comedy and tragedy. 'Aristotle has not defined pity and terror: I have', announces Stephen in *Stephen Hero*. On 13 August 1904 Stanislaus Joyce declares in his diary that James 'upholds Aristotle against his friends, and boasts himself an Aristotelian'. But the best demonstration comes in a letter from Joyce to his brother in 1903, about a meeting with John Synge. Joyce recognized in Synge a distinct, and therefore competing, talent. Synge showed him *Riders to the Sea*, and Joyce (as he boasted to his brother) riddled it until it had not a sound spot left. 'Thanks be to God', he said in summary, 'Synge isn't an Aristotelian.' It was good luck that his foremost rival should not be strengthened by his favourite philosopher, thus leaving that corner to Joyce. Nor did his admiration fail: in Zürich, while writing *Ulysses* in 1919, he said to his friend Georges Borach that Aristotle was the greatest thinker of all time.

So much fondness for Aristotle may appear belated, but the whole of *Ulysses* is a triumphant anachronism. At the Bibliothèque Sainte-Geneviève, as Stephen echoes in *Ulysses*, Joyce himself read Aristotle 'night by night'. If he liked a writer he tried to read everything by him – a compliment he paid to Flaubert, Dante, Ibsen, and a few others. His writings show that he was familiar with major and minor works, not only the *Physics*, the *Metaphysics*, and the *Nicomachean Ethics*, but the *Problemata*, the *De Anima*, the *De Sensu*. The special relevance of this philosophy to Joyce in Dublin in the year 1904 was that he saw around him an idealism as rampant as Plato's. What he liked about Aristotle was that he had demoted Plato's Ideas, had denied that universals could be detached from particulars, and in short had set himself against mysticism. In Dublin Joyce observed his contemporaries bemused by the 'fairyland' which in his essay 'Drama and Life' he had already rejected. They saw a folk not a people, fairies not forces, folklore not engaged art. For philosophy they turned to occultism, to theosophy, to magic, all purporting to commandeer Private Matter by Sergeant Mind. Their metaphysics was linked to a belated aestheticism, in which beauty was sought as if it had being apart from material entanglement. To their eyes, it *floated*.

In rejecting Dublin metaphysics, Joyce knew he was at variance with Yeats. In an early pamphlet he had accused this poet, whom in other moods he immensely admired, of being an aesthete with 'a floating will'. He could not have approved of Yeats's essay, 'The Autumn of the Body', in which the poet (later to celebrate the body's springtime) said he had 'lost the desire of describing outward things, and found that I took little pleasure in a book unless it was spiritual and unemphatic'. Yeats went on to complain of the 'externality' which a time of scientific and political thought had brought into literature, and said that the arts were now going to fill men's thoughts 'with the essences of things, and not with things. We are about to substitute once more the distillations of alchemy for the analyses of chemistry. . . .' Joyce could not pass a chemistry course – he failed three times – but he did not take to alchemy either. Yeats was vulnerable, then, but Stephen never attacks him, only Mulligan does. It is a demonstration of a respect which Joyce yielded to no other Dublin contemporary.

Instead of Yeats, he made use of another prominent Dubliner, George Russell (AE), as target. Yeats's occultism was highly qualified, Russell's was straightforward. Russell thought all existence was Maya, and pursued reality by vision and invocation. William Schutte has recently discovered in a 1904 issue of *Dana* (the magazine that refused the first version of Joyce's *A Portrait of the Artist*), an essay by Russell in which he says, 'Spirituality is the power of apprehending formless spiritual essences, of seeing the eternal in the transitory, and in the things that are seen the unseen things of which they are the shadow.' It was against this shadow school that Joyce mobilized 'solider Aristotle', and in his broadside, 'The Holy Office', composed during his last summer in Dublin, he attacks the members in turn. While this poem has been read as a *jeu d'esprit*, Joyce meant every word:

> Myself unto myself will give
> This name, Katharsis-Purgative.
> I, who dishevelled ways forsook
> To hold the poets' grammar-book,
> Bringing to tavern and to brothel
> The mind of witty Aristotle,
> Lest bards in the attempt should err
> Must here be my interpreter:
> Wherefore receive now from my lip
> Peripatetic scholarship.

He mocks the visions of his contemporaries, and concludes:

That they may dream their dreamy dreams
I carry off their filthy streams
For I can do those things for them
Through which I lost my diadem,
Those things for which Grandmother Church
Left me severely in the lurch.
Thus I relieve their timid arses,
Perform my office of Katharsis.
My scarlet leaves them white as wool.
Through me they purge a bellyful.

Of course Joyce knew that the Dublin mysticists had not invented idealism. There was at least one idealist writer, William Blake, whom he admired as much as they did. While he was gathering himself to write *Ulysses*, he lectured (in 1912) on two writers, Blake and Defoe, the latter as respectful of matter as the former was contemptuous. The lecture on Blake is especially important because Joyce rarely expressed himself in any but fictional or poetic terms, and because, as he remarked to his brother, he put himself behind what he did. Much of Blake's thought he regarded as splendid error: 'Blake killed the dragon of experience and natural wisdom, and, by minimizing space and time and denying the existence of memory and the senses, he tried to paint his works on the void of the divine bosom.' Blake was a mystic, but not a mysticist. He 'unites keenness of intellect with mystical feeling', a quality 'almost completely lacking in mystical art'. And while Blake did say, as Russell said after him, that the vegetable world was but a shadow of eternity, he also said, in a sentence Joyce liked better, 'Eternity is in love with the productions of time.' As for the Dublin Blakeans, however, 'they creepycrawl after Blake's buttocks into eternity of which this vegetable world is but a shadow'.

Against them Stephen admonishes himself, 'Hold to the now, the here. . . .'

Joyce regarded the Dublin mysticists as in undisclosed collusion with the Catholic Church, which especially in Ireland, perhaps out of Jansenist lag, derogated the mortal body in favour of the immortal soul. But the disease was not restricted to one alone of the British Isles. Beyond the Irish Sea was an England dominated by Victorian pruderies, moneyed and aristocratically obtuse. The systematic malformation of life manifested itself in many ways, not the least important being attitudes to love. In 'The Holy Office' Joyce made an unexpected attack on female coyness as on male idealism; they were counterparts. The sugaring of love and courtship was a part, and not an inconsequential one, of the general self-deception and refusal to recognize reality. Against all such deceptions he displayed his own artistic banner, which, he told Gogarty, was 'Describe what they do'. For him the yogibogeybox could offer nothing so good as the vegetable world. Spirituality was a means of denial of the universe just as pernicious as Mulligan's lack of spirituality.

Like Margaret Fuller, Joyce could say, 'I accept the universe.' What the universe was had been laid down by Aristotle. Joyce found in Aristotle someone to whom he could go to school, for in *De Anima* Aristotle addressed himself to that very question of idealism versus materialism which to Joyce appeared basic. Aristotle rejected both positions. Against idealism, he declared that the soul was inextricably bound up with matter. He rejected the transmigration of souls, with which Joyce disports a little in *Ulysses*, on the ground that the soul is only the soul of its particular body and can't survive a transplant. He also specifically ruled out, as Stephen Dedalus does, the conception of one man's having a succession of souls. Stephen clings to western, Aristotelian notions of identity.

Aristotle also rejects solipsism or subjectivism: if a subjectivist says nothing, there is no use arguing with him – he is nothing but a vegetable; but if he can be made to say the word 'man', for example, then he can be forced to admit that he means something different from 'not-man'. The law of contradiction, which, Stephen declares, underlies all Aristotle's psychology, and which in turn underlies the first three episodes of *Ulysses*, prevents 'man' and 'not-man' from being the same thing. On the basis of such distinctions the non-subjective, external world can be built up in unchallengeable thereness. Mulligan's lumping together of human and animal, of Irishism and Irish sycophancy, of cruelty and kindness, are failures to acknowledge the law of contradiction. As he says, quoting Whitman: 'Do I contradict myself? Very well, I contradict myself.' Like Synge, Mulligan is no Aristotelian. On the other hand, against mere naturalism Aristotle insists that there are incorporeal things. And in *De Anima* he points out that the soul is the form of forms, because through the soul's form all other forms of things have to be known.

Stephen follows Aristotle faithfully enough in the first three episodes. The third, *Proteus*, begins with the resounding phrase, 'Ineluctable modality of the visible'. The word 'ineluctable' is polemically Aristotelian: there is no veil of Maya here, no cocoon of the self into which to creepycreep. If the phrase sounds overeducated, all the better from Joyce's view, since Stephen must be sharply differentiated in expression from Bloom and Mrs Bloom, who both agree with him about matter. He is here as artist, he says, to read the signatures of things, those ineluctable fusions of form and matter. His aesthetic does not float like that of the aesthetes. Stephen tests Aristotle's view of space and time by shutting his eyes. Will the world empty if the perceiver blots it out? If so, the subjectivists and the idealists are right. But he opens his eyes again and confirms Aristotle, though he humorously summons a doxological rather than a peripatetic phrase for the purpose: 'See now. There all the time without you: and ever shall be, world without end.' For Stephen as for Aristotle, Gautier's phrase holds true, 'I am one for whom the visible world exists.' At this point in the third chapter, Joyce put his belongings together and left Trieste for Zürich. The external world had been authoritatively posited and could be packed into his suitcase.

Even with help from Aristotle, Shakespeare, and Goethe, the *Odyssey* remained hard to reconcile with modern material. Some elements must at first have seemed unmalleable. The *Odyssey* takes place in three zones, heaven, earth, and the underworld. Earth and the underworld could be managed by a modern writer, but heaven offered difficulties. Joyce might have followed Homer, as Goethe did, by contriving a prologue in heaven; or he could like Hardy have convoked an assemblage of demiurges and spirits. But the bias of Joyce's book is so much in favour of human rather than superhuman life that these possibilities did not suit him. On the other hand, whenever a difficulty appeared, he embraced it. The Homeric gods *do* manifest a number of times in *Ulysses*, shaking the earth, wielding the thunderbolt; but for his principal movers and shakers Joyce adopted two undeclared gods of this world, space and time. These have their kinship to body and soul, temporal and spiritual power; but they also exert in most of the book a godlike influence on the proceedings.

This cosmic pressure is never acknowledged in Joyce's remarks about *Ulysses*, but in *Finnegans Wake* he avowedly makes Shem and Shaun, Earwicker and Anna Livia Plurabelle, the gracehoper and the ondt, the tree and the stone, the two washerwomen, into time- and space-types. In *Ulysses* the roles are apportioned rather to episodes than to characters. I shall propose that in every group of three chapters the first defers to space, the second has time in the ascendant, and the third blends (or expunges) the two. Space has priority because in each triad the external world has to be posited before it can be countered or undermined. So the first chapter in *Ulysses* is given over to space, which, as Stephen defines it later, is 'what you damn well have to see'. No structure could be more solidly spatial than the nine-foot-thick Sandycove tower. And in it is a solid man, Buck Mulligan, heralded by the adjectives 'Stately, plump'. Mulligan is occupied in spatial activity: he is endeavouring to give substance to the body and blood of Christ in the chalice of his shaving bowl, over which he has crossed his razor and mirror. The host is imperfect — Mulligan admits to a little trouble about those white corpuscles, a reference to the lather in the bowl. God's body is invoked verbally as well as sacramentally in this episode, always in terms of concrete entities: Mulligan speaks of God as 'collector of prepuces', and Stephen calls him 'chewer of corpses', a premonitory union of birth and death metaphors as of divine and human. Father, Son, and Holy Ghost become the three eggs which Mulligan, beginning *ab ovo*, slaps on the plates for breakfast. Under Mulligan's aegis of denial, godsbody becomes dogsbody.

The authority of space over the scene is asserted in the way that whatever is mentioned is quickly bodied. The sea is identified by Mulligan, with Swinburne's assistance, as the great sweet mother, then, in mock-deference to Homeric epithets, as 'the scrotumtightening sea'. To Stephen (as a cloud momentarily covers the sun), the sea is rather a bowl of green vomit, such as his mother coughed up in her last illness. For Mulligan the miracle of making wine at Cana is compared to making water, implying a blasphemous union of creation and decreation. His 'Ballad of Joking Jesus' renders spatial the timeless by turning Christ into a flying-machine. When a spirit does appear, Stephen's mother in his dream, she is not fleshless but wears her corrupted flesh. Ireland is embodied in the guise of 'a wandering crone', the old milkwoman. A more sombre denizen of this world is the imagined body of the man who has drowned, now being sought for off shore. Stephen's refusal to swim is in part a refusal to yield to the blandishments of space, which may also be regarded as the diversions of hell. He continues to deny the deniers.

Magpie and Cuckoo (2)

In the second chapter the sceneshifter is not space but time. Space had offered extension, time now offers succession. The episode begins with a history lesson, in which Stephen has to instruct his pupils about one of those bloody battles which in *Finnegans Wake* are dismissed as clashes of 'wills gen wonts'. This one is the battle of Tarentum, ambiguously won by Pyrrhus, and Stephen thinks that all victories in war are equally Pyrrhic. Two theories of history are at issue: Haines, apologizing for the British occupation of Ireland, had remarked to Stephen, 'It seems history is to blame', as if history were some demonic force; but Mr Deasy, headmaster of Stephen's school, has a different view: he holds with Hegel that 'All history moves towards one great goal, the manifestation of God.' (Deasy's attempts to make time divine are the opposite pole to Mulligan's effort to make God human.) Stephen ponders the two theories – of history as infernal and of history as divine – and he also considers Blake's pronouncement that history is fabled by the daughters of memory and so is a record of what never happened. He doesn't accept Blake's view, regarding it as motivated by impatience and couched in overstatement. Still, the idea roots itself in Stephen's mind, and he says, 'I hear the ruin of all space, shattered glass and toppling masonry, and time one livid final flame.' Wryly he asks, 'What's left us then?', that is, if space and time are destroyed. This question is to be answered at the end of the book. But for now Stephen sticks with Aristotle, and allows history to survive as 'an actuality of the possible as possible'.

Various aspects of time are marshalled in this chapter. Joyce builds on the contrast that Stephen as compared with Mr Deasy is young, but as compared with his pupil Sargent is old. Politically, Deasy lives in the past, frozen in Ulsterite frenzy. Financially, Deasy puts away for the future. What he offers to Stephen, as worldly wisdom, is archaic conservatism in politics, and conserved wealth in finance – kingdoms of the past and of the future. Stephen seeks a different kingdom, that of the 'now, the here'. And so he counters Deasy, and Haines as well, by announcing that 'History is a nightmare from which I am trying to awake.' The evidence of this wakefulness is his debts, which testify to his attempt to live in the present, unconscionably it may be, but desperately. Better debts than battening upon past and future. An I.O.U. is an act of moral defiance.

In this episode, Joyce examines history in two modes, secular and spiritual, Caesar's and Christ's. The battles of Tarentum and Asculum – Caesarism – Stephen thinks of as 'Jousts, slush and uproar of battles', and counterposes them to Christ in 'Lycidas', described by Milton, also in terms of power, as 'the dear might of Him that walked the waves'. Stephen speaks of Christ's shadow as lying upon us all. This contrast is posed again in Mr Deasy's two collections, of Stuart coins and of apostle spoons. Physical and spiritual might, empire and church militant, battle for our bodies and souls. Mr Deasy, senile warrior, cries, 'I will fight for the right till the end', and dodders on, 'Ulster will fight. And Ulster will be right,' like a mockery of all nationalism. He is a carrier of the world's lunacies.

In Caesar, Stephen finds a history of oppression of the Irish; in Christ, oppression of the Jews. Mr Deasy sees no incompatibility in regarding the manifestation of God as history's goal, and in endorsing anti-Semitic persecution. The two powers, secular and spiritual, are related in that both depend upon cruelty. Stephen will render nothing unto God or Caesar, for nothing is really theirs. Wars are equally destructive whether they are fought for secular or spiritual motives. And Stephen mentally equates the two collections of Stuart coins and apostle spoons with Deasy's third collection, which is of shells. Hollow shells are what sacred and profane relics alike come to.

Against them he proclaims Aristotle's definition of the soul from *De Anima*: 'The soul is in a manner all that is: the soul is the form of forms. Tranquillity sudden, vast, candescent: form of forms.' The essential virtue of the soul is not embattlement but freedom. Physical history–wars, and spiritual history–wars too, are alike opprobrious to him.

Stephen accepts that the past has existed, but he refuses to allow its dominion over the present. These shells are to be trodden under foot, not held in veneration. There is another way of taking in the past, but it is not identified until later.

Why Stephen Dedalus Picks his Nose (3)

If the corruptions of space dominate the first episode, and the corruptions of time the second, the third chapter is Stephen's attempt to sort out corrupt and incorrupt. Joyce emphasized that this chapter was protean and had change for its theme, but it is also about permanence and identity. The identity is both of persons and things: they are observed in their pristine strength and in their dissolution, aborning and adying.

Stephen's long monologue appears at first to be totally improvisatory in organization, but it has an underlying structure. At the beginning Stephen abstracts the categories of space and time from the universe, as to some extent Joyce has done, and tests them as if he were their first manufacturer. Then he makes the experiment I have mentioned of closing off the external world of space by shutting his eyes and living altogether in the internal world of time. But the space world is not so easily dismissed.

This episode, like all the rest, is broken by a caesura, which here occurs when Stephen changes the direction of his steps. The first part deals with what is primal, the second with what is terminal. In the first part Stephen, after creating or at least recreating the material world, observes two midwives with a bag, and these make him ponder his own creation, then the creation of Adam and Eve, and then the conception and birth of Christ. The mystery of paternity, because so remote from the act of giving birth, occupies him more than motherhood, and he ruminates on true fathers, ghostly fathers, church fathers, and father priests who in chalices throughout the world bring God once more to birth. His thoughts about women's role in creation also extend from Mary to Eve to Magdalen to the moon.

But after he turns from the Pigeonhouse road, Stephen thinks of the dissolution of matter. He observes the carcass of a dog, and imagines what the corpse of the drowned man will look like when fished up. He imagines woman with her demon lover, death. It is noon, yet for the moment he sees not the brightness of the sun but the darkness of his shadow. If his shadow were endless (that is, if he were no longer bound by space and time), would it still be his? The implicit answer is no, because mortality suffuses his every thought. His words, he thinks, are becoming dark, and he imagines himself saying to a girl, 'Darkness is in our souls, do you not think?' 'Days make their end', he concludes sadly, and acknowledges that 'Evening [death] will find itself in me, without me.'

A single process binds the two parts of the episode, birth and death. This is not growth but corruption. Stephen sees all created things in process of decay, every day dying a little, as if death were a concurrent process. Many examples congregate in his mind. There is the decay of his house, of his father's family and his uncle's. Men like Swift have gone mad. Marriages are broken up. Even heaven has not escaped, for allbright Lucifer has fallen from it. (Dante, just before he leaves the Inferno, is also shown the place in it where Lucifer fell.) As for God, his transformations are a series of falls: 'God becomes man becomes fish becomes barnacle goose becomes featherbed mountain.' All life sinks in the wet sand like Stephen's boots: 'Dead breaths I living breathe, tread dead dust.' Birth is bound to birth by corruption: he imagines death coming to kiss a girl, mouth to her mouth, to her womb: 'allwombing tomb'. He had announced at the beginning of his monologue that he was here to read the signatures of 'seaspawn' and 'seawrack', and seawrack obsesses him now. In accordance with this mood, he urinates, expressing one form of corruption. He feels his nose full of mucus, another form, and picks it. He feels his decaying teeth as earlier he had savoured his decaying house.

Besides generation and corruption, another element is hinted at in this episode. The monologue begins, after all, with Stephen reading, and it ends with his writing a poem, adding his signature to the signatures of all things. The poem expresses the marriage of contraries, *Tod und das Mädchen*, 'He comes, pale vampire . . . mouth to her mouth's kiss.' As against the seduction poem in *A Portrait of the Artist*, 'Art thou not weary of ardent ways,/Lure of the fallen seraphim', this is a poem of revulsion, yet somehow assimilating the revulsiveness into rhythm and rhyme. While Stephen was urinating in the Cock lake (there really is a Cock lake on Sandymount strand), the sound was verbalizing in 'wavespeech'. He longs for the 'word known to all men', and will later fruitlessly ask his mother what it is. Even the sands are 'language tide and wind have silted here'. Art too has its place in creation-destruction, to voice its basic processes, which Stephen's poem expresses as love and death.

Stephen urinates to anticipate the 'urinous offal from all dead'; he picks his nose for that reason and for another as well. Like Joyce in 'The Holy Office', he sees it as his heroic duty to carry off all the filthy streams, to acknowledge corruption. He has a more abstract purpose too. Not having found a handkerchief in his pocket, he is obliged to proceed bravely without one, and announces, 'For the rest let look who will.' But to belie his nonchalance, he suddenly says, 'Perhaps there is someone', and looks quickly behind him. This backward glance is a parting denial of the subjectivist universe which briefly attracted him at the beginning of the episode, as well as of the universe of moribund gloom which has filled his thoughts. Since Stephen is an artist, Joyce implies that art is not self-isolation, that it depends upon recognition of other existences as well as one's own.

What Stephen sees, in this munificent gesture, is not a person but a ship; it is the *Rosevean*, 'homing, upstream, silently moving, a silent ship'. Ships have female names but this one seems androgynous, like *Le France* or the ship in *Finnegans Wake* which is named the *Bey for Dybbling*. In this third chapter, which synthesizes its predecessors, the sexes interfuse, and the sea, until now the great sweet mother, is hailed as Father Ocean. The ship does more than help reconcile the sexes, however; it endorses man's enterprise, binds him to nature, countervails Stephen's thoughts of dissolution and decay. The *Rosevean* seals the marriage of form and matter, of body and soul, of space and time, at which Aristotle had officiated.

II

Browne and Nolan

Since Joyce's entire book was to take place in Ithaca, in Ithaca*novant*, Homer's sails had to be reefed as feet. Within one city it would be necessary to match the geographical adventurousness of Telemachus' voyage to Nestor and Menelaus, and Odysseus' voyage by raft to Phaeacia. Joyce accepted from Homer the double quest, son searching father and – to sharpen Odysseus' aim – father searching son. In fact, the double plot of the two searches became the theme of much of his book, though not to the exclusion of other themes. To demonstrate the degree of parallelism, Joyce devised three episodes about Bloom to cover the same hours, from eight to twelve, already covered in Stephen's day.

He had next to decide how close the parallels should be. He had created his two principals as more kind than kin, and he intended that they should move figuratively towards 'fusion' (as he said in the Linati schema) in a way that members of the same family, imperfect copies of each other, could not. He was aware that the two characters might exploit not only various models, but the separation which middle age had brought home to him personally, since the insurgent bachelor, oriented towards departure, had become perforce the husband-father, oriented towards homekeeping. Accordingly he could have conceived of Bloom and Stephen as two octaves, a musical analogy glossed by Stephen in the *Circe* episode as 'reduplication of personality'. But Joyce wished his characters to have lives of their own apart from his life.

Therefore Stephen, much more than Bloom, is made conscious of himself as an existential person, a separate and distinct being whose every act is crucial. His daydreams also establish him as an isolated figure: 'I just simply stood pale, silent, bayed about', he thinks to himself on Sandymount strand. This self-involvement is different from Bloom's firm sense of the objective world; what books and brooding do for Stephen is done for Bloom by observable reality. One is inward bound, the other outward. In temperament Bloom balances Stephen's edgy, recalcitrant mind by abundant goodwill. Stephen's temptation is Luciferian subjectivism, and Bloom's is too generous a concession of other people's otherness. Stephen is like Wallace Stevens's Crispin, at the stage when he still holds that 'Man is the intelligence of his soil,/ The sovereign ghost', while Bloom responds to Crispin's later formulation, 'His soil is man's intelligence'. Stephen abrades while Bloom is, except in crisis, convivial; Stephen is coercive and Bloom uncoercive.

These differences lead to others which are worked out with the same attention. Stephen ponders metaphysics, Bloom physics. Stephen speculates about the soul, while Bloom – to whom soul is brain and grey matter – ponders on the body. Stephen is obsessed by questions of the relative degrees of ghostliness and substance in the persons of the Trinity; he lumps them together under the rubric of 'contransmagnific-andjewbangtantiality' (the consubstantiation, transubstantiation, magnification of a Jewish, explosively begotten God-man). To Bloom, as to Wittgenstein, such questions are neither answerable nor askable. Wraiths do not torment Bloom in the way that the ghost of Stephen's mother besets Stephen. In *Exiles* Joyce makes Robert summarize the difference between himself and Richard as that Richard has fallen from a higher world and he has risen from a lower one. Stephen and Bloom have performed the same acrobatics.

Bloom being the principal figure, he is more immediately accessible than Stephen. He is not afraid that he will compromise his selfhood, nor does he fear as Stephen does that by concession he may start up a pernicious chemical action in his soul. Joyce's intentions regarding Bloom have sometimes been misconstrued. Bloom is exceptional rather than average. As Joyce said to Budgen, Bloom is a good man. A youthful essay in which Joyce, quoting Parsifal, asked, 'Who is good?', indicates that he did not offer this accolade lightly. The goodness was not goodygood; Bloom, Joyce told another friend, was *gutmütig* rather than *gut*. Unassuming goodness was the variety he was prepared to endorse. Moreover, he intended Bloom to be a complete man. When Budgen, invited to play devil's advocate, offered Christ as a more complete hero, Joyce held his ground: 'He was a bachelor, and never lived with a woman, surely living with a woman is one of the most difficult things a man can do, and he never did it.' Budgen proposed Faust, and Joyce replied, 'No-age Faust isn't a man. . . . Is he an old man or a young man? Where are his home and family? We don't know. And he can't be complete because he's never alone. Mephistopheles is always hanging round him at his side or heels.' Hamlet was the next nomination. Joyce rejected him as only a son. 'Ulysses', he said,

is son to Laertes, but he is father to Telemachus, husband to Penelope, lover of Calypso, companion in arms of the Greek warriors around Troy and King of Ithaca. . . . Don't forget that he was a war dodger who tried to evade military service by simulating madness. He might never have taken up arms and gone to Troy, but the Greek recruiting sergeant was too clever for him and, while he was ploughing the sands, placed young Telemachus in front of his plough. But once at the war the conscientious objector became a jusqu'auboutist. When the others wanted to abandon the siege he insisted on staying till Troy should fall. . . . And then he was the first gentleman in Europe. When he advanced, naked, to meet the young princess, he hid from her maidenly eyes the parts that mattered of his brine-soaked, barnacle-encrusted body. He was an inventor too. The tank is his creation. Wooden horse or iron box – it doesn't matter. They are both shells containing armed warriors.

Joyce wished Bloom to be heroic as well as good and complete. In his early essay, 'Drama and Life', he declared that a measure of heroism could be elicited from the vulgar circumstances of everyday life just as from the days of clanking mail. The task was to exhibit heroism of a new kind, undistinguished by any acts, distinguished maybe by the absence of act; Bloom, like Richard in *Exiles*, does nothing, though he influences others. Yet he must be separated from those about him, and by the gift of expression – the highest a writer can bestow on his creature. It was easy to separate Stephen because of his extraordinary cultivation. But Bloom has to speak in ordinary language, untrained by anything but natural ingenuity, relaxed rather than tense, not so fastidious as to be above the most wellworn expressions, yet sceptical of them, even taking a keen pleasure in manœuvring among common idioms, allusions, and proverbs. It is this power of speech, mostly inward speech, that inclines Bloom towards Odysseus – resilience, the power to recoup in the mind what he loses in the flesh.

It might appear that Bloom, however Odyssean, lacks

Stephen's prime characteristic, the artistic sense. But Joyce implies otherwise. He makes Bloom display a considerable if untutored interest in drama and fiction. Bloom likes *Hamlet* and finds no difficulty in liking also Mosenthal's *Leah*; he feels no compulsion to rank these two favourites in order of merit. When in the privy he reads 'Matcham's Masterstroke' he is not moved or touched by it – these are his criteria – but he is impressed by its slickness and dreams of emulating it. Perhaps he will write a story about a proverb, and sign it 'By Mr and Mrs L. M. Bloom' (a curious surrender of his own second initial – P. for Paula – in favour of his wife's first one). In the past, as Bloom recalls, he has jotted down bits of his wife's conversation with the notion that they might in themselves compose some kind of literary work. In fact these entries bear a crude resemblance to the inch-by-inch naturalism which Stephen Dedalus at moments practises, and also to the jumpiness of the internal monologue. For Joyce's purposes an unimaginative Bloom would not have done at all, since so much of the book was to take place within his mind.

The trio of episodes about Bloom begins with the one that Joyce labelled *Calypso*. His plan had been to allow the three episodes of the *Telemachiad* to present a world in abstract patterns. In one of his schemas for *Ulysses* Joyce wrote that Stephen in the first three episodes does not yet bear a body, and it seems appropriate that in Stephen's universe of *no* he should have none, while Molly Bloom's fullbodied universe (in the monologue at the other end of the book) should be pervaded by *yes*. Stephen is still engaged in 'lordly study' and remains abstract. In so far as he is corporeal he is only incipiently so. He is allowed nine episodes, as an embryo is allotted nine months, to move from potentiality to realization.

Middle Earth (4)

A different role is reserved for Bloom, who has bodiliness to spare. Stephen must move from the abstract to the concrete, Bloom reverse the procedure. Bloom's inclinations before breakfast are visceral. His brain is full of body, his mind – as he busies himself in the kitchen – full of kidneys. At the butcher shop he observes the nextdoor girl and aspires to walk behind her moving hams. He thinks of her big policeman friend and comments, 'They like them sizable. Prime sausage.' Throughout this episode a relation is established between humans and their food, a relation of interchangeability. Women have hams, men sausages. The cat confirms, by his easy intimacy with Bloom, the bond between animals of different species. His anus, noted on the chapter's first page, evokes Bloom's, on the last.

The whole sensory world is mustered for this episode. Bloom is all eyes and ears, tastebuds, nostrils, fingers, as he starts the day. Instead of an abstract discussion of colour by Stephen, with allusions to Aristotle and Berkeley, the spectrum rainbows the chapter. Bloom, from the moment he is seen moving 'about the kitchen', is all movement, up and down stairs, off to the butcher and back, up and down stairs again, off to the privy, moving his legs, arms, jaws, and finally bowels. The kidney appears both as an image in his mind and as a real object; he turns it over in his head as he turns it over in the frying pan later, he thinks of the living animal from which it comes, contemplates it in its butchered state, buys it, cooks or rather overcooks it, puts it on a plate, eats, digests, and finally excretes it or something like it, and considers its final use as fertilizer.

Beyond these examples, everything depends upon physicality in *Calypso*. The imperfections that one puts up with in daily physical life are suggested by the humpy tray and the broken commode. Molly Bloom is, for this hour, an exclusively physical presence. She is reading a book, however – surely this is an intellectual act, we might presume – but no, it's a pornographic book, and it lies next to the orangekeyed chamberpot, and close to her warm body, the weight of which disturbs the quoits of the bed when she moves. She asks for another book, specifying it should be by Paul de Kock, a further contribution to the episode's bodiness.

The chapter is also one of solids, planted on the solid earth. There are allusions to heat, to weight, to the sunlight and shadow which warm or cool them. Most of the physical imagery refers to internal organs, as if to pursue the kidney down the body. Joyce also developed the spatial implications of the episode, as in the first episode about Stephen: *Calypso* compiles layers of substance, though it considers them under the aspect of the dance of the hours, of movement in time.

Naming the fourth episode *Calypso* strained Homeric analogy. In what sense might Molly be both the immortal nymph Calypso and the mortal Penelope? Homer did perhaps unconsciously offer a hint in making both women into weavers. Joyce's intentions may be discovered from a letter to Harriet Weaver (his truest Penelope), from internal evidence, and from the Linati schema. He wrote Miss Weaver, who had complained that the *Penelope* episode was posthuman, that he would accept this word so long as prehuman was added to it; as against Penelope, he intended the more human apparitions to be Calypso, Circe, Nausicaa, and others. In the Linati schema Joyce lists 'nymph' as one of the episode's symbols, and a picture of the bathing nymph presides over the lectual activities of Molly Bloom. Bloom considers that it is quite like his wife when she was slimmer. It would seem that Calypso represents one aspect of Molly, her physical presence; she is someone to be thought about, written to, explained to, observed, fed. In another manifestation, Molly is a subject (rather than a direct or indirect object), charged as firmly as Bloom or Stephen with the duty of contemplating and evaluating her world. Joyce reverses Homer in making Calypso less deific than Penelope. In the role of Calypso, Molly is unfaithful. Bloom has to proceed from this version to her more intrinsic character as Penelope, from mistress to wife. But Joyce had another idea as well. In the lost epic, the *Telegony*, the sixth-century B.C. continuation of the *Odyssey* by Eugammon of Cyrene, Odysseus after his return to Penelope is off again on a voyage which takes him to Thesprotia. There he marries the queen, who is named Callidike. In the Linati schema Joyce surprisingly lists Callidike as one of the characters in *Calypso*. In a sense, then, *Ulysses* must have seemed to him to be the further adventures of Odysseus. Whenever confronted by a choice between two possible things to include, Joyce chose both. It was natural that he should have wished to embrace both Odyssean and post-Odyssean wanderings. After all, Ulysses must come to Dublin.

For many promptings, as Gilbert makes clear, Joyce depended upon Victor Bérard's attempt to locate the supposedly mythical topography of the *Odyssey* in actual places. Bérard finds much of his evidence in proper names, which he traces to their roots. Etymologically the name Calypso is related to Calpe, meaning pitcher or bowl, and Calpe's mount is Gibraltar. Homer says that Calypso lived in 'a navel of the sea', an island, and Joyce clearly derived from this the idea that

Stephen's first chapter, parallel with this one, should have a navel too – the *omphalos* tower, and a bowl as well – the bowl of vomit next to Mrs Dedalus on her deathbed, which is reiterated in the shavingbowl and the sea – another 'bowl of bitter waters'. Joyce may also have felt confirmed in what must already have been his intention, of giving Molly a Gibraltar childhood.

In the *Odyssey* Hermes is sent to Calypso as Athena to Telemachus, and bears a message from Zeus. She is enjoined to give up Odysseus and send him on towards Ithaca. (Athena, as the old milkwoman, reminds Stephen of his race, and so of the conscience he has promised to forge for it.) Calypso, whose name means 'the Concealer', does not inform Odysseus that she has received this message, but she suddenly offers to help speed his departure instead of preventing it. Joyce found resonance in the fact that Calypso is secretive, and he imitates Homer by a series of secret messages. The most obvious one is postal, Blazes Boylan's letter, which by an unHomeric twist informs Calypso of her new lover's advent rather than of her old one's departure. Molly follows the nymph's example in not divulging this letter's contents to her heroic husband. There are other secret messages: one is written in Greek, the word 'metempsychosis', which Molly is reluctant to understand though she is in process of metempsychosis from Penelope to Calypso to Callidike and back again. Bloom's faltering explanation specifically mentions nymphs as something the Greeks believed one could be changed into. Other secret messages are exchanged between Bloom and the cat. But a more important one is transmitted to Bloom at Dlugacz's butcher shop: Bloom realizes from the Zionist leaflet (Agendath Netaim, a redevelopment project in Palestine, with headquarters at 34 Bleibtreustrasse, Berlin) on Dlugacz's counter, that Dlugacz, porkbutcher or not, is a Jew; their eyes meet in sharp recognition, as Calypso at once penetrated Hermes' disguise, being a goddess herself, to spot him as a god. Bloom receives this message but decides to go into the matter another time.

The most Olympian messages are those which come to Bloom from the heavens, first by the agency of a cloud, then by the agency of the sun. He has let his mind dandle Palestine as the promised land, crowded with olive trees, citrons, oranges. Though not a Zionist – he considers Dlugacz an enthusiast and has an eighteenth-century suspicion of enthusiasm as of superstition – he feels a slight sympathy: 'Nothing doing. Still an idea behind it.' But a moment later a grey cloud covers over the sun, the same cloud which made Stephen see the ocean as a 'bowl of bitter waters'. Bloom deflates Zionism as Stephen elsewhere deflates Irish causes. The promise of the promised land has long since been broken:

> No, not like that. A barren land, bare waste. Volcanic lake, the dead sea: no fish, weedless, sunk deep in the earth. No wind would lift those waves, grey metal, poisonous foggy waters. Brimstone they called it raining down: the cities of the plain: Sodom, Gomorrah, Edom.

(Edom is a mistake, like Bloom's later lumping together of Peter Carey the informer and Peter Claver the missionary, or his reference to the eulogy in a country churchyard by Wordsworth or Campbell; these are bloomisms, a form as distinct as spoonerisms or malapropisms. A bloomism is an uneasy but scrupulous recollection of a factual near-miss. Since it often involves similar sounds as well as similar facts, the whole of *Finnegans Wake* is implicit in it.)

All dead names. A dead sea in a dead land, grey and old.
Old now. It bore the oldest, the first race.

At this point an old woman passes in front of him like a
human cloud, and Bloom's thoughts darken more:

> A bent hag crossed from Cassidy's clutching a naggin bottle
> by the neck. The oldest people. Wandered far away over all
> the earth, captivity to captivity, multiplying, dying, being
> born everywhere. It lay there now. Now it could bear no
> more. Dead: an old woman's: the grey sunken cunt of the
> world. [61; 73]*

It is characteristic of Bloom, and of this chapter, to find in a
part of the body, especially an internal organ, an image of
personal desolation. It is also like Bloom to seek refuge from
such thoughts in another physical image: 'Be near her ample
bedwarmed flesh. Yes, yes.' And as if to sanction this wish,
the cloud lifts and another messenger arrives, the sun:

> Quick warm sunlight came running from Berkeley Road,
> swiftly, in slim sandals, along the brightening footpath.
> Runs, she runs to meet me, a girl with gold hair on the
> wind.

(Another thought from Berkeley – the philosopher – had a
similarly optimistic message for Stephen earlier.) This image,
gold as the rod of Hermes which Calypso admires so much,
in part because it is the colour of her own tresses, is the
opposite of the bent hag and the old milkwoman, prior

* Bracketed page references following extended quotations from *Ulysses* are
to the two standard editions, the one published by Random House, New York
(1934) and the other by The Bodley Head, London (1937), cited in that order.
There are several reprints with different pagination, of which the Penguin
Modern Classics edition (London, 1969) is the most recent.

messengers from the secret morning, and it brings Bloom out of despond and leads to his return home. Here Calypso shifts for a moment into Penelope, as Molly becomes, from a caverned, idle, and secretive nymph, the redemptive object of Bloom's journey. As an image the girl with gold hair is grandiloquent, but Joyce was willing to risk her so as to match the aureal splendour of Hermes.

The dialectic of the two images in Bloom's mind, of Zion and Sodom, may be illustrated:

Zion	*Sodom*
Bleibtreustrasse	[Untreustrasse]
Palestine heavenized	Palestine infernalized
Beautification (enthusiasm)	Uglification (dumps)
The Perfect	The Horrid
False Life (Heaven)	False Death (Hell)

Empty Images

Antidote

Molly's 'ample bedwarmed flesh'
Fidelity/Infidelity
Earthly Paradise
(Middle Earth)
Non-Zionist/Non-Sodomist

That Other World (5)

Because of the triadic arrangement of the book, the second episode in each triad must play truant to the first. Compulsions take over from tasks, madness from order. Having voyaged down the alimentary canal in *Calypso*, Joyce chose a different kind of 'trip' for the *Lotus-Eaters*. If *Calypso* is predominantly in space, the *Lotus-Eaters* is predominantly in time; the eaters have in fact all the time in the world, but it is time observed under the aspect of space, that is, in a series of almost still pictures of stilled movements (or at least slow-motion ones) and hushed appetites.

If *Nestor*, the parallel episode, is full of past history and outdated ideas, the Lotus-Eaters live in a prolonged present, divorced from history not because they have awakened from its nightmare (as Stephen is avowedly trying to do) but because they have put it to sleep. Joyce might have done the whole chapter in the languorous style of Tennyson's *Lotus-Eaters*, but this would have been to forget that Odysseus must evade them, and so in the midst of temptations to be irresponsible Bloom's mind darts as nimbly and undefeatedly as ever. In his outward conduct, however, he is affected by them enough to slow down.

The episode contrasts with *Calypso* in several ways. In place of *Calypso*'s emphasis on internal organs, this chapter offers external ones, specifically, as Joyce said, the skin. Instead of the vagina it dwells upon the penis. *Calypso* joined human and animal flesh, food and excrement, the *Lotus-Eaters* joins the human and vegetable worlds through drugs and metaphors. Most conspicuously, flowers and petals stand as botanical equivalents of skin and external organs, a point specified by Joyce in his final image of Bloom's penis prefigured as a languid floating flower in the bath. The union of men and plants is also suggested by the human use of nicotine, opium, and other vegetable substances.

Scorning the solid food and waste of *Calypso*, this chapter furnishes liquids. From Bloom's mind the kidneys have flown, and in their place great barrels of porter have been delivered:

'Barrels bumped in his head: dull porter slopped and churned inside. The bungholes sprang open and a huge dull flood leaked, flowing together, winding through mudflats all over the level land, a lazy pooling swirl of liquor bearing along wideleaved flowers of its froth.' (Froth is the skin of porter.) Liquid consonants are also favoured, *l* sounds – for languor, lolling, floating – as opposed to strong consonants and purposive acts.

Calypso had offered a gamut of sensory stimulants, the *Lotus-Eaters* offers a gamut of anaesthetics. Mouth has its cigarette, lollipop, communion wafer, wine, tea, liqueur (horsemouth has oats), body its perfume, head its hairoil, nose its ragpaper and scented soap smells, eye its mild erotic spectacles, ear its music, Latin, and bells, mind its fancies, penis its womb of warmth (the bath) and its gelding (the horses). In *Calypso* the East, as imagined by Bloom, was a place where robbers roamed and mothers called their children home, but in the *Lotus-Eaters* the East is marked by no such brisk activities, it is *dolce far niente*.

This opposition is heightened by the two letters, one from Milly Bloom in *Calypso*, the other from Martha Clifford in the *Lotus-Eaters*. They are both excellent, in their respective and contrasting kinds. Milly writes her father,

> Dearest Papli,
> Thanks ever so much for the lovely birthday present. It suits me splendid. Everyone says I'm quite the belle in my new tam. I got mummy's lovely box of creams and am writing. They are lovely. I am getting on swimming in the photo business now. Mr Coghlin took one of me and Mrs will send when developed. We did great biz yesterday. Fair day and all the beef to the heels were in. We are going to lough Owel on Monday with a few friends to make a scrap picnic.

Give my love to mummy and to yourself a big kiss and thanks. I hear them at the piano downstairs. There is to be a concert in the Greville Arms on Saturday. There is a young student comes here some evenings named Bannon his cousins or something are big swells he sings Boylan's (I was on the pop of writing Blazes Boylan's) song about those seaside girls. Tell him silly Milly sends my best respects. Must now close with fondest love.

    Your fond daughter,   Milly.

    P.S. Excuse bad writing, am in a hurry. Byby. M.

                                      [65–6; 79–80]

Milly's letter belongs to the world where objects, people, cluster, congregate. It is full of obvious and obtuse feelings about clothing, candy, young men, people around her. Her expressions – 'beef to the heels' (for plump farmers' wives), 'getting on swimming in the photo business', have an inept force. She has so much to do, so many plans, is in such a hurry. Martha Clifford lives under a different star; her letter is addressed to Bloom under his *nom de plume* of Henry Flower:

    Dear Henry,

    I got your last letter to me and thank you very much for it. I am sorry you did not like my last letter. Why did you enclose the stamps? I am awfully angry with you. I do wish I could punish you for that. I called you naughty boy because I do not like that other world. Please tell me what is the real meaning of that word. Are you not happy in your home you poor little naughty boy? I do wish I could do something for you. Please tell me what you think of poor me. I often think of the beautiful name you have. Dear Henry, when will we meet? I think of you so often you have no idea. I have never felt myself so much drawn to a man as you. I feel so bad about. Please write me a long letter and tell me more. Remember if you do not I will punish you. So now you know what I will do to you, you naughty boy, if you do not write. O how I long to meet you. Henry dear, do not deny my request before my patience are exhausted. Then I will tell you all. Goodbye now, naughty darling. I have such a bad headache today and write *by return* to your longing

MARTHA.

P.S. Do tell me what kind of perfume does your wife use. I want to know.

[76–7; 94–5]

Martha likes money, not work; perfume, not picnics. Instead of Milly's heartiness Martha is all stale air and innuendo, with nothing definite, not even her name or Henry's. Milly's errors in composition come from youth and impatience and lack of training, Martha's are examples of grammatical decay, of language gone gamey. For the moment she is Bloom's Calypso.

Bloom's adventures in Lotus Land include two meetings, one with C. P. M'Coy and the other with Bantam Lyons. These differ from his meeting with Dlugacz in *Calypso*, which resulted in the purchase of the all-important kidney, in being non-events. Bloom tries to get rid of M'Coy, says he is going 'Nowhere in particular' for fear that, if a destination is stated, M'Coy will offer to accompany him; anticipating a well-known manoeuvre of M'Coy to borrow a valise for his wife's putative concert tour, Bloom announces that his own wife is also touring. (M'Coy and his wife, whose voice has 'No guts in it', are Lotus Land replicas of Bloom and Molly.) M'Coy doesn't ask, and Bloom doesn't refuse, the scene being static. Entreaty and denial are alike unspoken, still Bloom has dodged past this peril. As for Bantam Lyons, he hopes for a tip on the race, thinks he has received one from Bloom for Throwaway, but is deluded – Bloom has offered nothing and doesn't approve of gambling.

The episode begins with deceptive indulgence. Passing a boy smoking a cigarette butt (another external organ), Bloom thinks of reproving him but then reflects, 'O let him! His life isn't such a bed of roses!' But, after rejecting lotophagous temptations, he is less indulgent towards Lyons's betting mania, which comes at the chapter's end: 'Regular hotbed of it lately', he complains. Bloom feels throughout the chapter a morning torpor, nowhere to go and nothing to do, floating mentally from the Dead Sea to his anticipated bath. 'This is my body', he thinks of the latter image, and the Christlike words point up how Bloom has translated a miracle into a natural 'phenomenon' (a favourite word with him). The analogy between chalice and tub is clearly intended, Bloom being not divine bachelor but by vivid hyperbole progenitive human, father of thousands. It is a counter-image also to Christ's walking on the waves. Joyce prefers the human form divine to the divine form human. He chose man occasionally surpassing himself rather than a god sporadically slumming on earth.

Though lured by self-surrender, Bloom does not give way. He meditates on two religions, of East and West, Buddhism and Christianity:

Same notice on the door. Sermon by the very reverend John Conmee S. J. on saint Peter Claver and the African mission. Save China's millions. Wonder how they explain it to the heathen Chinee. Prefer an ounce of opium. Celestials. Rank heresy for them. Prayers for the conversion of Gladstone they had too when he was almost unconscious. The protestants the same. Convert Dr William J. Walsh

D.D. to the true religion. Buddha their god lying on his side in the museum. Taking it easy with hand under his cheek. Josssticks burning. Not like Ecce Homo. Crown of thorns and cross. [78–9; 98]

Buddha lolls while Christ writhes, permissiveness as against discipline, abandon versus sacrifice of self. But Bloom has a further idea about this opposition: he discovers in it a secret identity. Both religions are narcotic. Christian penance, Bloom finds, has its own lusciousness. He may be wrong, but this is his contribution to theology, and one which his creator does not discountenance. The meditation reads like a commentary on Mulligan's bowl of lather, over which a mirror and a razor lay crossed: narcissism and cruelty over sentimentality equal religion. 'Confession. Everyone wants to. Then I will tell you all. Penance. Punish me, please.' He plays here on Martha's lubricious suggestion that she might punish him. There is a pleasure in confession, 'Lovely shame', he calls it. He watches the priest administering the sacrament, and its reception is at once confectionary, sexual, and cannibalistic:

The priest bent down to put it into her mouth, murmuring all the time. Latin. The next one. Shut your eyes and open your mouth. What? *Corpus.* Body. Corpse. Good idea the Latin. Stupefies them first. Hospice for the dying. They don't seem to chew it; only swallow it down. Rum idea; eating bits of a corpse why the cannibals cotton to it. . . . Now I bet it makes them feel happy. Lollipop. . . . There's a big idea behind it, kind of kingdom of God is within you feel. . . . Safe in the arms of kingdom come. Lulls all pain. [79–80; 98–9]

As if to foreshadow his interpretation, he has thought about a holy picture of Martha and Mary listening to Christ, of two sluts he heard singing a bawdy song about 'O, Mary lost the pin of her drawers . . .' and of his own Martha and Mary (Marion):

> Martha, Mary. I saw that picture somewhere I forget now old master or faked for money. He is sitting in their house, talking. Mysterious. Also the two sluts in the Coombe would listen.

Religion appeals equally to the holy and debauched. In this mood Bloom imagines meeting Martha Clifford one Sunday after the rosary, and in a further speculation, links gelded horses and eunuch choir singers: 'Suppose they wouldn't feel anything after. Kind of a placid.' '. . . might be happy all the same that way.' Self-mutilation, like religious self-denial and penance, is a perverse pleasure, a form of narcissism.

For this kind of lotus-eating, or other kinds, Bloom has no appetite. This is the first episode where he encounters his world (though he has been skilful with Molly earlier) and for the moment he is content with brilliant evasion. He skirts bravely self-denial and self-surrender, on a bypath which might be called (borrowing a phrase used in another connection by Stephen) 'almosting it'. He prefers what Augustine termed 'morose delectation' (dwelling upon impure thoughts), a sin to which Stephen humorously owns in the *Proteus* episode, and which plays a mighty role in this book. Bloom's reaction to Martha Clifford, another Lotus-Eater, is to continue the letter-writing, not to see her. He knows too well what would happen if they met: 'Usual love scrimmage. Then running round corners.' He will not bring Lotus Land into his active life; a penpal is better than a bedpal.

In this chapter some actions are prevented by choice, some by accident: Bloom would have liked to look at the ankle of the girl getting up into her carriage, but he succeeds only in almosting it. He almost remembers the law of falling bodies, almost gives away his newspaper, almost mentions Boylan's painful name, almost buys Molly her lotion. At church he will not pray, any more than Stephen will, but he will eye the churchgoers and inspect them as anthropological specimens. (In the next chapter he genuflects but doesn't pray.) It is proper that the chapter should end not in an actual bath, but in the dream of a bath. (It parallels Stephen's daydream of a drowned man.) Stephen would not swim, and neither does Bloom, but Bloom can contemplate in prospect water covering his body, not in the hope of a spiritual but only of a physical cleansing. So he avoids the rigour of spiritual purges and of refusals to undergo them.

The Circle Joined (6)

Having established Bloom's scepticism towards both secular and spiritual uplift, towards Jewish nationalism and Christian regeneration, Joyce had next to bring to a climax the second triad of episodes. The sixth episode was particularly important because it concluded the separate movement of Bloom and Stephen: hereafter they begin, unconsciously at first, to work together rather than apart. Joyce chose to place at this point the descent to Hades, which was pivotal for Odysseus as well, since it was in Hades that he learned his eventual fate and that of his companions. More than this, it was a sudden, solemn change of perspective, the only part of the *Odyssey* where the seafaring hero goes underground.

Joyce took up this challenge by situating his episode in Glasnevin cemetery; there as in Hades the denizens are dead and the living are interlopers. No ghosts rise, though the 'memory of the dead' is sharp and clear. Because this chapter parallels *Proteus*, Joyce establishes a subtle counterpoint. At the beginning of his protean walk Stephen had seen the midwives who might have officiated at his birth; at the beginning of his funeral ride Bloom observes an old woman peeping from behind a blind, and thinks of her as one who prepares a corpse for burial. Stephen broods on the navel cord which binds us all, he says, to the Garden of Eden; Bloom broods on the coffin band which binds us all equally to Tophet. Stephen's perplexity over Christ's two fathers achieves its parallel in his having himself two fathers in Simon Dedalus and Bloom; but Joyce is able to solve this confusion by setting the two fathers side by side in the funeral carriage. It is the first time in literature that this problem has been overcome, as well as the first time it has been posed. At the end of *Proteus* Stephen has a mental image of the drowned corpse, and Bloom balances this by an image of a corpse decaying on land. Both heroes have to face the reality of death, as Odysseus faced it before them.

They also think about women. For Stephen women are distant creatures, changeable as the moon and to be seen mythically as great sources of fertility and corruption. His is young men's thinking; women are for him still objects, as the Women's Liberation Movement complains, largely unknown objects, idealized or brutalized in the imagination. Bloom has a different view. Against *la donna è mobile* he sings *le donne son stabili*. Women, not woman, interest him. He knows personally, or knows about, all the women who pass through his mind in comparable procession to Stephen's mostly unknown 'She, she, she'. Bloom's interest is in women unmythed and actual. Even Martha Clifford, whom he has never seen, possesses in his mind's eye a non-mythical quality different from that of Stephen's mental images. Bloom figures out, for example, that Martha's headache is probably menstrual. In this contrast Joyce is cavorting with the difference between men who have lived with women and men who haven't. As Blake wrote, 'When a man has married a wife he finds out whether/Her knees and elbows are only glued together.' Stephen has not yet found out.

The difference may be summarized more grandly in their disparate views of Queen Victoria; for Stephen she has been amusingly described by a French journalist as the 'old hag with the yellow teeth'. He is content to leave her at that. Bloom thinks of her as a widow like the widow Dignam, and comments,

> Widowhood not the thing since the old queen died. Drawn on a guncarriage. Victoria and Albert. Frogmore memorial mourning. But in the end she put a few violets in her bonnet. Vain in her heart of hearts. All for a shadow. Consort not even a king. Her son was the substance. [101; 128]

He dimly echoes here Stephen's speculations about ghostliness and substance: 'Something new to hope for not like the past she wanted back, waiting. It never comes.' This is a kindlier vision.

What Joyce wishes to display are Bloom's iron affections for the dead he has lost, and especially for his son Rudy and his father, whose death day is to be celebrated in a week's time. Joyce intends that Bloom should anatomize death more completely than Stephen, and so he does, with wary sympathy. He considers the death of husband or wife, and notes,

as might La Rochefoucauld, that the surviving partner may
have some satisfaction as well as grief in outliving the other.
He recognizes that Paddy Dignam, although his friends say he
was 'as decent a little man as ever wore a hat', is not to be
greatly missed. Beyond such practical insights, he insists that
it is folly to pamper the dead, whether in the Egyptian or
Christian way: 'They're so particular. Lay me in my native
earth. Bit of clay from the holy land.' Burial customs interest
him when they express or seek to express affection: 'Only a
mother and deadborn child ever buried in the one coffin. I
see what it means. I see. To protect him as long as possible
even in the earth. The Irishman's house is his coffin. Em-
balming in catacombs, mummies, the same idea.' Faced with
the panoply of mourning, he concludes, like Wallace Stevens,
'Let *be* be finale of seem.' Walking past the 'saddened angels,
crosses, broken pillars, family vaults, stone hopes praying
with upcast eyes, old Ireland's hearts and hands', he is firm:
'More sensible to spend the money on some charity for the
living.' Bloom's views have their force because so interfused
with sympathy.

Joyce intends that Bloom should separate himself deci-
sively from Christian conceptions of death. Learning that
Dignam has died of a heart attack, he says, 'The best death',
regardless of his fellow-mourners' regret that there has been
no time for the last rites. When they say nothing, he insists,
'No suffering. . . . A moment and all is over. Like dying in
sleep.' He does not mind their disapproving silence; it is his
first declaration of independence. Joyce had inverse authority
for this scene in the *Odyssey* where, when Odysseus com-
pliments Achilles on being a potentate even in Hades, Achilles
curtly replies, 'Don't bepraise death to me, Odysseus. I
would rather be ploughman to a yeoman farmer on a small

holding than lord paramount in the kingdom of the dead.' In
a comparable moment at the cemetery, Mr Kernan praises
the Protestant service as simpler and more impressive than
the Catholic, and quotes, '*I am the resurrection and the life.*
That touches a man's inmost heart.' Bloom politely pretends
to agree, but his thoughts diverge:

> Your heart perhaps but what price the fellow in the six feet
> by two with his toes to the daisies? No touching that. . . .
> Once you are dead you are dead. That last day idea. Knock-
> ing them all up out of their graves. Come forth, Lazarus!
> And he came fifth and lost the job. Get up! Last day! Then
> every fellow mousing around for his liver and his lights and
> the rest of his traps. Find damn all of himself that morning.
> Pennyweight of powder in a skull. Twelve grammes one
> pennyweight. Troy measure. [104; 133]

The deadness of the dead rouses Bloom to eloquence.

Joyce allows Bloom to look more and more closely at
death, and as he does so an internal tension mounts in him
and in the episode. Nondescript Paddy Dignam's death will
do as well as any other to elicit lamentation and horror. As
the funeral car drives towards Glasnevin, it passes Reuben J.
Dodd, who gave the boatman a florin for rescuing his son
from committing suicide by drowning. 'One and eightpence
too much', comments Simon Dedalus, and the value (or
valuelessness) of life is brought home. The mourners pass the
house where Childs perhaps murdered his brother. They are
hard on suicide, all except Bloom whose father has died in
that way. At the cemetery are so many graves, of Mrs
Dedalus, of Daniel O'Connell and Parnell: 'How many!'
thinks Bloom. 'Faithful departed. As you are now so once
were we.' In Bloom's imagination the dead begin to speak

as once they did for Odysseus in Hades, but less portentously. He imagines a gramophone in the grave or kept in the house, the record of the deceased played to the bereaved on ceremonial occasions.

Having rejected bodily resurrection, Bloom has to confront bodily dissolution. The dead fertilize the living: 'It's the blood sinking in the earth gives new life. . . . Well preserved fat corpse, gentleman, epicure, invaluable for fruit garden.' He contemplates decay in detail: 'Rot quick in damp earth. The lean old ones tougher. Then a kind of a tallowy kind of a cheesy.' He sees an obese grey rat going into a crypt, 'Tail gone now', and reflects that

> One of those chaps would make short work of a fellow . . . . Wonder does the news go about whenever a fresh one is let down. Underground communication. We learned that from them. Wouldn't be surprised. Regular square feed for them. Flies come before he's well dead. Got wind of Dignam. They wouldn't care about the smell of it. Saltwhite crumbling mush of corpse: smell, taste like raw white turnips. [113; 145]

This is about as close a view of the charnel house as any writer has given. In the *Lotus-Eaters* Bloom disported with the pleasures of the body, here he faces up to the horror of its dissolution.

He pulls himself together as he moves towards the glimmering gates. These are no longer the gates of Dis; they might be the gates of what Stephen called the 'allwombing tomb'. 'Back to the world again. . . . I do not like that other world she wrote. No more do I. Plenty to see and hear and feel yet. Feel live warm beings near you. Let them sleep in their maggoty beds. They are not going to get me this innings. Warm beds: warm fullblooded life.'

The way back to life is not totally pleasant for Bloom, any

more than it was for Odysseus, since he experiences a snub from the solicitor Menton near the cemetery gates, much as Odysseus had to put up with the refusal of Ajax, nursing an old grudge too, to speak with him in Hades. Warm fullblooded life is no paradise. But Ulysses is strengthened in convictions about death and life, determined to go on: 'Well, I am here now.'

To be here now meant to be a twentieth-century man in the world as well as in Ireland, and Joyce so interpreted it. Although he spoke less and less of his political concerns, he felt them deeply, and they help to articulate the skeleton of *Ulysses*. For this book, as later for *Finnegans Wake*, he drew upon the historical and philosophical theories of Giambattista Vico, which Croce had been making better known while Joyce was living in Trieste. *Finnegans Wake* begins by a reference to the Vico road in Dalkey, a topographical feature which Joyce obviously considered symbolic, and another reference to this road appears in the second chapter of *Ulysses*. Joyce followed Vico but at his own pace; he held, as Vico did not, that the best political system was the democratic one. But he embraced eagerly Vico's cycle of three ages, theocratic, aristocratic, and democratic, concluding in a *ricorso* and another cycle. The *ricorso* was not so much a turnabout, as a promotion from experience to experience comprehended and known. Joyce said in a letter that the theory had amply demonstrated itself in his life, and quite possibly he saw himself as having begun in fear of God, then basking in family and personal pride, and finally, dispossessed, discovering a sufficient value in the ordinary and unassuming. That, at any rate, is the grace shadowed in *Ulysses*.*

* Ellsworth Mason, in an unpublished doctoral dissertation at Yale in 1948, first detected the Vichian aspect of *Ulysses*. I find the relation of Vico's ages to Joyce's book to be different, after the first six chapters, from what which Mr Mason urges.

Specifically, the pattern helps to animate the two triads with which *Ulysses* opens. The first chapter begins with a mass and ends with a priest, and its equivalent in Bloom's experience, the fourth, begins with the steeple of George's church and ends with its 'high up' bells. The second and fifth chapters play different variations on the theme of aristocracy, as Stephen teaches at a rich boys' school and listens to the headmaster discourse of princes and kings' sons, and as Bloom ogles an aristocratic lady about to get up into her carriage, then ponders on the ways of the Anglo-Irish Trinity College and the Kildare street club. In the third and sixth chapters both Stephen and Bloom take a more democratic view; Stephen utters good doctrine when he says, 'You will not be master of others or their slave', and Bloom finds an apt parable in the democracy of death. Seen in this Vichian light, the sudden appearance of the ship *Rosevean* at the end of *Proteus* heralds a change, a *ricorso*, a reformulation of Stephen's state. At the end of *Hades*, Bloom emerges from the Stygian darkness to ascend through the gates to a kind of new birth, which is substantiated by the imagery of *starting* and of *delivery* at the beginning of the seventh chapter.

But for the principal context of the first six chapters, Joyce depended upon the man whom he valued as 'the father of what is called modern philosophy'. He awarded this title, in a review in 1903, to Giordano Bruno. Bruno more than anyone probably enlarged Joyce's perspective beyond Aristotle. The strange history of Bruno, his brilliant career, his visit to England and friendship with Sir Philip Sidney, his heresy and its punishment by burning, were bound to excite Joyce's sympathy. Bruno was in fact named, simply as 'the Nolan' (he came from Nola, near Naples, and was proud to speak of himself this way), in 'The Day of the Rabblement', the pamphlet which Joyce published privately in 1902: 'No man, said the Nolan, can be a lover of the true or the good unless he abhors the multitude'; the next year Joyce wrote of Bruno as the 'most honourable' among the 'vindicators of the freedom of intuition'. Bruno appears in the last pages of *A Portrait of the Artist* as well as in *Finnegans Wake*. Joyce did not respond to the Hermetic side of Bruno, which has recently excited much interest; but he respected his unAristotelian passion, his 'ardent sympathy with nature as it is – *natura naturata*', his mystical faith in interconnection as a world-principle.

Bruno did not supersede Aristotle in Joyce's mind, but was superimposed upon him. Aristotle's ethical theory of a mean between excess and defect still held, but Bruno proposed an emphasis on the kinship of contraries as facets of the same entity. (Aristotle acknowledged that excess and defect were often closer to each other than to the mean, but Bruno was much more insistent.) Ultimately, said Bruno, all contraries are coincident. Hot is opposite to cold, but they are both aspects of a single principle of heat, and their kinship can be seen in the fact that they are united at their minima, the least hot being also the least cold. The deepest night is the beginning of dawn. Bruno declares that love is hate, hate love, that poison yields its own antidote. For Joyce this was no finespun theory, but an axiom which he saw everywhere confirmed. It helped him to organize *A Portrait*, which begins with the birth of the body and ends with the birth of the soul.

Giordano Bruno's coinciding contraries may in retrospect be seen to give form to each episode of *Ulysses*, as though each had been generated out of some pair of seeming opposites which might be shown to join. The first episode registers the secret affinity of sacredness and damnation as

Mulligan administers communion and, a fallen Lucifer, calls himself Jesus. He pretends to be the complete iconoclast but is indignant with Stephen for not having outwardly conformed. Though irreligious, he serves the church, just as, though pretending to be an Irish nationalist, he toadies to British imperialism. In the second episode, Judaeo-Christianity and Caesarism show an astonishing likeness in that the Romans and Jews persecute the Jewish Christ and both Romans and Christians persecute Jews. In the third chapter the sea as creative mother is joined with the ocean as destructive father, birth with death.

In the three chapters involving Bloom, Joyce again follows Bruno. The first joins food and faeces which will one day be food once more. The second finds Christ and Buddha, self-discipline and self-abandonment, to be essentially the same. In *Hades* Bloom reminds us, as Stephen reminded us earlier, that in the midst of life we are in death.

But Joyce was not satisfied to use Bruno's coinciding contraries only thus far. Each of the first three chapters is half a circle, to be completed by its parallel chapter in the second triad. Mulligan's transubstantiation of God into flesh in *Telemachus* is completed by Bloom's transubstantiation of flesh into faeces (*Calypso*). The sadism of Christians and Romans persecuting Jews (*Nestor*) is completed by the masochism of Christians and Buddhists in their devotions (*Lotus-Eaters*). In the *Proteus* episode Stephen follows the arc of generation through corruption to death, while in *Hades* Bloom begins with death and follows it back to birth. 'Who does not see', says Bruno, 'that there is a single principle for corruption and generation?' Mother-sea and father-ocean, whom Stephen had joined, are matched by Bloom's implicit coupling of mother earth and fatherland. Birth-death and death-birth join like land and water. The lying in of birth coincides with the laying out for death.

Beyond these circles, Joyce established a larger enclosing circle of Bloom and Stephen. Disparate as they at first appear, they are made to join more and more closely in their attitudes towards life, Stephen denying its deniers, Bloom affirming directly. They match each other's views of death, religion, nationality. Both pursue a mean between pure mind and mindlessness, mere body and bodilessness. Their spiritual kinship, which is eventually to make them putative son and father, is postulated firmly by the end of the *Hades* episode. Joyce hinted as much by making the circle the geometrical symbol of *Hades*, as Gilbert pointed out without recognizing its meaning. It was in fact the maker's seal upon the first six episodes.

Bruno's doctrine did not loom so large for Joyce simply as a mechanical convenience. He was exalted by it, for it meant that nothing was isolated. Bruno's contraries coincide to confirm their mutual participation in Being, 'the foundation of all kinds and of all forms'. Being is what Wallace Stevens calls 'the ever-never-changing same'. 'Thus everything which maketh diversity of kinds, species, differences, properties, everything which dependeth on generation, corruption, alteration and change is not being or existence but is a condition and circumstance of being or existence which is one, infinite, immobile, subject, matter, life, soul, truth and good.' By Bruno's theory everything is contained as in a seed or, as Yeats wrote when he completed his own visionary account of being,

> All things hang like a drop of dew
> Upon a blade of grass.

III

Harsh Geometry

In about the year 1937 Joyce had his friend Eugene Jolas read aloud to him W. B. Yeats's symbology of life, art, and death, *A Vision*. Jolas reports his comment, 'What a pity he did not put all this into a creative work.' Joyce probably knew that Yeats had suffused many poems and plays with this visionary material, but his reproach supposed a possible book of much larger scope. What prompted his remark was the recognition of the easy convertibility of Yeats's abstract symbology into actual symbolism, a recognition that came easily because the 'harsh geometry' of *A Vision* bore extraordinary resemblances to the equally harsh geometry which formed the marrow of *Ulysses*.

The sense that he had used so complicated a structure sometimes troubled Joyce. 'I may have oversystematized *Ulysses*', he remarked in an unguarded moment to Samuel Beckett. Having attempted a work comparable, in complexity at least, to *The Divine Comedy*, he could not be sure that his novel, or any novel, might bear such freight. He oscillated between attesting elaborateness and minimizing it.

The preceding chapters have moved closer and closer to another schema of the first six episodes different from the two that Joyce sent to Linati and Gilbert. In it, the episodes are juxtaposed in such a way as to emphasize their parallelisms. The elements furnished here are provisional, or rather partial; they have to be completed by others which will make themselves felt in later episodes.

TELEMACHIAD – BLOOMIAD

Episode	Contraries	Coinciding by	Product	Presiding category	Dominant symbol	Vichian parallels
(1) Telemachus	Divine/Human Spirit/Matter God/Man Godsbody/Dogsbody	Transubstantiation	Jesus, Host, Food	Space	Martello tower (military)	Age: Theocratic Language: Sacred-Greek, Irish Wisdom: Oracular (Delphic *omphalos*)
	Wine/Water Razor/Mirror (Cruelty/Narcissism)	Absorption Intersection	Urine Christianity			
	Church/State	Collusion	Subjugation			
(4) Calypso	Human/Animal	Digestion (Transubstantiation)	Faeces	Space	George's Church (militant)	Age: Theocratic Language: Sacred-Greek, Hebrew Wisdom: Oracular (solar and nubilous)
	Bloom/Molly	Sympathy	'Mr and Mrs L. M. Bloom'			
	Penelope/Calypso	Metempsychosis	Wife–mistress			
(2) Nestor	Human/Marine Caesarism/ Christianity Stuart coins/ apostle spoons Age/Youth	Simplification Will to power (over others)	Hollow shells Persecution (sadism)	Time	Body supernatural (Christ putatively walking on water)	Age: Aristocratic (rich boys– kings' sons) Language: Symbolic-poetry Wisdom: Devious (Stephen with Deasy)
	Deasy/Stephen Stephen/Sargent	} Parallax	Son–father			

		Surrender	Masochism	(Bloom in bath — water — imagined)
	Sacred and Profane Love Penis/Womb Flower/Water Host/Chalice Christ/Buddha Self-sacrifice/Self-abandonment Penis (castrated)/Penis (uncastrated)	Immersion Asceticism Stultification	Bath of male in tub (female) Loss of identity Torpor	Language: Symbolic-opera (Italian) Wisdom: Devious (Bloom with M'Coy)
		Generation–Corruption	Death-in-life	Space–Time
(3) *Proteus*	Birth/Death Mother-sea/Father-ocean Fecundity/Sin Divine/Human Descent		Allwombing tomb God-man	Navel cord Noon and (imagined) evening
				Age: Democratic Language: Vernacular (Dante, gipsy, wave-speech) Wisdom: Sympathetic *Ricorso* (1–3): Ship
		Corruption–Generation	Life-in-death	Time–Space
(6) *Hades*	Death/Birth Corpse/Earth Coffin/Hole Fatherland/Mother earth Laying out/Lying in Age/Youth Bloom/Rudy } Virag/Elcom } Human/Divine Parallax Ascent		Birth Father-son Man-god (*Outis*–Zeus) (Odysseus)	Coffin band (Imagined) midnight and dawn
				Age: Democratic Language: Vernacular (Irish anecdotes, donkey bray, gramophone) Wisdom: Sympathetic *Ricorso* (4–6): Birth

Three Propositions

From the circles of the first six episodes three unstated propositions declare themselves. Their ontological validity is established not by the philosophical authority of Aristotle or Bruno, but by the simple force of recognition. The book as image demands these glosses as registers of its meaning.

The first proposition sets forth the workings of the spirit of denial. According to it, (I) *secular power and spiritual power egg on their adherents to persecute others and to abase themselves.* Imperialism, which can be religious as well as profane, is in either aspect missionary for hatred although it pretends, through father-figures such as king, priest, fatherland, to proffer paternal love. *In the church militant, as in Caesarism, the Marquis de Sade and the Freiherr von Sacher-Masoch are conjoined.* Their ultimate expression is Nobodaddy, as Blake called the tyrant god, and Noboddady may only be overcome by imaginative sympathy. The distinguishing marks of this sympathy are furnished by Bloom and Stephen in their completion of each other's thought.

Against the reign of denial and hatred nature also offers a recourse. The second proposition begins with Stephen's gloomy view that (II) *the newborn experiences corruption and dies*; then adds Bloom's sanguine corollary, that *having died, the being experiences corruption and is in some manner newborn.* 'April's green endures.'

The final proposition is more complex. (III) *God, descending, becomes flesh becomes food, is eaten, becomes faeces, then becomes food becomes flesh becomes man ascending.* That is, the obverse of God's descent into matter is matter's ascent towards at least provisional divinity. Joyce, unlike Dostoevsky, prefers man-god to god-man. He thinks of his hero as man-god, and finds for Odysseus a supporting etymology – that the name is formed from *Outis* (no one) and Zeus. Man is the divine nobody, he emerges from the nondescript as Henry Flower from Poste Restante. The powers of this world and of that other world try to keep this Bloom from blooming. They must be shown to fail.

IV

The Beast with Two Backs

Blowing Up Nelson's Pillar (7)

'In old days men had the rack. Now they have the press,' said Oscar Wilde. After the funeral hush of Glasnevin the scene shifts to noise and newspapers. In the mighty heart of the seventh city of Christendom, and in its lungs, there stands or rather used to stand – Joyce's Dublin is increasingly confined to his books – Nelson's pillar, ambiguously the sign of an empire's glory and, as Professor MacHugh says, of the defeat at Trafalgar of Europe's Catholic chivalry. In the *Aeolus* episode the din is portentous: earpiercing trams are being ordered to start from the pillar to all parts of Dublin, assuring corporal communication in the 'metrollops' (as *Finnegans Wake* jumbles it); mail vans bearing the royal initials are busily ensuring postal communication; while, more convivially, Guinness's men deliver barrels of stout to sustain oral communication. Municipal, national, and private enterprises send out their waves of power. But at the episode's end all three are in sudden arrest, 'becalmed in short circuit' like Odysseus' ships. In *Ulysses* a short circuit has long implications.

'The Mockery of the Victory' is the meaning which Joyce, in his schema sent to Linati, ascribed to this episode. It is a chapter of great exploits – conquests in the field, on the podium, in the press, at the bar. The celebrants of such conquests are like the suitors in the *Odyssey*, and Joyce manœuvres Homer for his purposes by combining the maritime combats of Odysseus with the hostilities of the *Nostos* (Return). Bloom and Stephen must take the city of Dublin, as if it were Ithaca. (There is even a suggestion of its being Troy, for, as someone says later of Bloom, 'He's a bloody dark horse himself.') Homer lurks in the background, providing Joyce with the god Aeolus, but Joyce arranges that the god should be flouted by the hero himself rather than merely by his crew.

Joyce is so far faithful to Homer as to let the initial burden of opposing the suitors fall principally on Telemachus. In the third triad of chapters Bloom is conspicuous only in the middle, Stephen holding the stage in *Aeolus* and *Scylla and Charybdis* with his two parables, one of nationalism, the other of art. In accordance with their hypothetical juncture in the first six episodes, the two men are now banded together without being aware of the fact. Unconsciously they are in league against the powers of this world and the next. Their first joint enterprise is in defence of language, both of English as a whole and of the integrity of each word. If the artist is to bring the word to his race, he must begin by rejecting false diction and the false gods it enshrines.

Bloom inconspicuously sets the pace: he first goes into the newspaper office, a penetration as symbolic as that he makes later into the maternity hospital. Once in, he observes the entrance of the newspaper publisher, William Brayden, and is abstractedly studying Brayden's fat neck when Red Murray whispers in awe, 'Don't you think his face is like Our Saviour?' To which Bloom, unawed, responds, 'Or like Mario.' Mario, a famous tenor of an earlier day, saved the scene in a hundred operas. Bloom's mind runs merrily over

the idea of 'Jesus Mario' singing *Martha*, a name with over-
tones for him both sacred and profane. Not yet fended off,
Red Murray announces, 'His grace phoned down twice this
morning.' His grace was William J. Walsh, Archbishop of
Dublin, quick to put pressure on the press. To this per-
sistence Bloom replies, 'Well, he is one of our saviours also',
and receives in reply, 'a meek smile'. Having released these
two arrows, Bloom continues his irreverent sharpshooting to
himself, 'But will he save the circulation?' The names of
power, Brayden, Jesus, the Archbishop, are suddenly col-
lapsed.

Murray's reverent confusion of the Lord with the press
lord is the other side of the Archbishop's attempt to make
the *Freeman's Journal* and *Evening Telegraph* accommodate the
Church's position. Bloom's first comment adroitly reduces
Brayden from a supernatural to an operatic figure, and his
second comment mockingly offers the same office of sal-
vationist to Brayden and Walsh, pressman and churchman.
(He anticipates the drunken cry in *Oxen of the Sun*, 'Shout
salvation in *King* Jesus.') Though seemingly haphazard, these
remarks neatly supply one of the keys to this episode, the
other being furnished subsequently by Stephen.

That the episode has keys is emphasized by the ludicrous
advertisement which Bloom is attempting to arrange for a
publican named Keyes. By picturing the crossed keys surrounded by a circle which constitute the insignia of the lower
house of the Isle of Man's parliament, Keyes means to demonstrate laboriously his latent sympathy for Irish Home Rule.
But in view of the recent appearance of the Glasnevin gates,
which open murkily to death and birth, and the sudden noon
light of Dublin at the beginning of *Aeolus*, it would seem that
the keys must open the gates of the city and of being. They

are also the two keys needed to unlock the gates of Purgatory in Dante, for the rest of this middle section of the book is purgatorial. The image is repeated in *Finnegans Wake* with Anna Livia's final cry, 'The keys to. Given.' Here in *Aeolus* Joyce is less threnodic though equally clamant. Bloom and Stephen possess the means of opening the locked city, even though they are ostensibly keyless, Stephen having surrendered his key to Mulligan, Bloom having forgotten his. Being themselves keys, their keylessness does not matter.

After Bloom initiates the action, Joyce has Stephen carry out the suggested strategy. He never allows Bloom to be relegated, however, and repeats, with variations, the outlines of the *Odyssey*. Aeolus' floating island, engirt with bronze, is volatile newspaperdom, engirt with steel presses and other hard substances, a blend of mutability and durability. The role of the god Aeolus is filled in part by the printing press, which cranks out on steel tablets its potent ephemera with sublime, godlike indifference. The machine has for regent Myles Crawford, editor of the *Evening Telegraph*, an irascible man who is tractable at Bloom's first appearance but at his second, like Aeolus with Odysseus, loses his temper. Since Joyce has added Telemachus to the scene, Stephen too must experience editorial rebuff. Under a favouring wind Crawford invites him to contribute a piece to the newspaper, 'Something with a bite in it', but on hearing Stephen's 'Parable of the Plums', Crawford conspicuously fails to renew his offer. He bears out Bloom's opinion that newspapermen are weathercocks.

Joyce needed an ethical parallel for Aeolus' fondness for six sons and six daughters, whom he has married to each other, and it appears in Crawford's incestuous admiration for his fellow journalists. He praises inordinately the 'scoop' by

which Ignatius Gallaher circumvented censorship and succeeded in telegraphing to a New York newspaper the escape
route used by the Phoenix Park murderers in 1882; his
enthusiasm evokes no response from the company except the
sponger Lenehan's 'Clamn dever'. On the other hand, the
timidity of the supposedly free press is italicized when Crawford, hearing Stephen speak of two old women raising their
skirts, offers the humorous caution, 'Easy all . . . no poetic
licence. We're in the archdiocese here.' Evidently Archbishop Walsh does not ring up the paper for nothing: priest
and pressman have their secret understandings.

Against Stephen and Bloom Dublin sends out three sorties,
in the form of set speeches. The first is that given by Dawson,
a baker, in the city council, reported verbatim in the morning newspaper. Dawson descants on the high trees of the
Irish forests and the serried mountain peaks and the mild
mysterious twilight with the moon above. (In this episode
height is an index of rodomontade.) Bloom thinks to himself,
'Bladderbags', and hearing a bit about 'our lovely land',
asks 'Whose land?' Nature-worship is not for him, any more
than for Blake. Rousseau's appetite for mystical nature is also
not requited here. The other Dubliners present are themselves embarrassed by Dawson, but they lend their support to
the next two sorties.

Before these are spoken, Joyce complicates the scene by
enlarging and shrinking its context, as if in sympathy with
Aeolus' bagged winds and their release by Odysseus' men.
Professor MacHugh offers a lofty contrast of Greece and
Rome, the former characterized by the New Testament, the
latter by new imperialism. The first is inspired breath, the
second expired carbon dioxide: '*Kyrie eleison*' versus Rome's
sewerage system, which MacHugh relates to England's pen-

chant for water closets. It is Lord Jesus versus Lord Salis-
bury, he says, Europe's Catholic chivalry versus Admiral
Nelson. The sponger Lenehan musters up a comparable contrast in his riddle, 'What opera is like a railway line?' The
answer joins *The Rose of Castille* with rows of cast steel, an
idiotic reduction of MacHugh's Greco-Roman antithesis to
bathos. Bathos (agent of truth) keeps butting into the bladderbags as the editor is interrupted in his praise of Gallaher
by the telephone bell, by the jutting up of his shirt dicky, by
the importunacy of Bloom. Unstoppable, Crawford tells off
Bloom (the true father) and perorates by calling Gallaher the
'daddy' of all the great pressmen of the day. In a book
ordinarily kind to daddies, this particular paternity is im-
pugned by Lenehan's hearty seconding, 'The father of scare
journalism . . . and the brother-in-law of Chris Callinan.'

Dawson's oratory has been deliberative, and the next
oration, as Joyce reminded Linati and Gilbert, is forensic.
This is the speech of the barrister Seymour Bushe in the
Childs murder case. It is declaimed with pomp by the seedy
barrister O'Molloy and evokes a Renaissance glory along
with a courtroom triumph. (The newspaper headlines move
forward through the history of modern journalism, while the
speeches move backward towards antiquity.) O'Molloy
begins with an error, probably calculated by Joyce, in mis-
placing Michelangelo's Moses in the Vatican instead of in
Santa Maria dei Vincoli:

> He [Bushe] said of it: *that stony effigy in frozen music, horned*
> *and terrible, of the human form divine, that eternal symbol of*
> *wisdom and prophecy which, if aught that the imagination or the*
> *hand of sculptor has wrought in marble of soultransfigured and*
> *of soultransfiguring deserves to live, deserves to live.* [138; 177]

This noble period is a cut above Dawson's, not nearly so doughy and aiming at sculpt. Stephen meditates, however, that Moses must have been 'a man supple in combat', but in this rendering is 'stonehorned, stonebearded, heart of stone'. (In *A Portrait*, against Cranly's 'grand manner', Stephen is 'supple and suave'.) It is ancestor- or hero-worship, blatant as Dawson's nature-worship. Its fustian is marked by ostentatious pairing of phrases long since drained of meaning. To speak of Moses' cornute-headed torso as 'the human form divine' glosses over a mystery and makes petrified absurdities of gods and men. The relevance of this high-flown Mosaic image to the law of evidence in the murder trial never appears. It is, after all, only wind. Following his recitation of Bushe's speech, O'Molloy seeks out Stephen to ask what he thinks of the hermetic crowd, the opal hush poets, and AE the master mystic. But his own declamation is as detached from reality as theirs, being all lifeless stone as theirs is lifeless apparition, both coinciding as hot air. Living tissue is the antidote to both.

The third speech, by John F. Taylor, is a public oration in defence of the Irish language revival, and here Dublin makes its strongest offensive. Joyce improved somewhat on the approximate version of the speech which was printed in a pamphlet early in this century. That he valued it is indicated by his having chosen it as the subject of his own gramophone recording of *Ulysses*. It has a passion and mordancy which Dawson and Bushe could not command. It leaves Rousseau and the Renaissance behind to return to the beginnings of Judaeo-Christianity. MacHugh is not allowed to recite it without interruption: there is his own belch of hunger, and Stephen's unspoken comment, 'Noble words coming', and 'Dead noise', which he ironically relates to the mystical idea of Akasic records or the *anima mundi* – a celestial newspaper 'morgue'. If orator's past glories were what Dublin needed, Taylor's speech was a glory of the orator's art:

> – But, ladies and gentlemen, had the youthful Moses listened to
> and accepted that view of life, had he bowed his head and bowed
> his will and bowed his spirit before that arrogant admonition he
> would never have brought the chosen people out of their house of
> bondage nor followed the pillar of the cloud by day. He would
> never have spoken with the Eternal amid lightnings on Sinai's
> mountaintop nor ever have come down with the light of inspiration
> shining in his countenance and bearing in his arms the tables of
> the law, graven in the language of the outlaw. [141; 181]

To these highsounding phrases Stephen's only response is to offer to buy everyone a drink. As the group leaves the offices and proceeds to Mooney's pub, there is a caesura, to signal a change of tone.

It might seem that Taylor is to go unchallenged, but actually Bloom has already set the strategy of counter-attack. In ruminating earlier about Passover, Bloom was reminded by the way printers read backward of how his father used to read the Hebrew of the Passover service. 'Pessach. Next year in Jerusalem. Dear, O dear! All that long business about that brought us out of the land of Egypt and into the house of bondage *alleluia*.' This bloomism is motivated by his unsentimental perception that Moses did not free the Jews from bondage, that – as he pointed out earlier in the day – they have gone from captivity to captivity. The analogy drawn by Taylor between Jews and Irish will not sustain a confidence in the national mission of either people.

Dawson's nature-worship, and Bushe's ancestor-worship, are resumed here with the utmost sonority. The professor remarks to Stephen of Taylor's speech, 'It has the prophetic vision. *Fuit Ilium!* The sack of windy Troy.' But Stephen refuses to accept the equation of windy Egypt and windy Troy, or of Canaan and Ireland. Jews and Irishmen may be compared – Joyce is always doing so – but not on this inflated level. Taylor's is a trumpery enthusiasm, a desire not to live in the present but to live in a petrified past and speak a dead language. Stephen now prepares to try Ulysses' great bow against this swollen windbag and the two smaller ones (Dawson and Bushe) beside it. 'I have a vision too', he tells MacHugh. He knows he will run afoul of their 'dead noise', but he prods himself, 'On now. Dare it. Let there be life.' This original commandment outweighs the ten that followed it. In *A Portrait* Stephen has said, 'Let the dead bury the dead.' Against Doughy Dan's ascent of the mountaintops and Moses' ascent of Mount Sinai, against nature- and hero-worship, he offers here the ascent of another high place, the man-made Nelson's pillar (an admiral to balance a general), by two present-day Irishwomen. The weapon of attack is art – 'PEN IS CHAMP' says a headline; the mode he chooses is naturalism – things as they objectionably are – expressed in a style graceless but also windless, without figures of speech. 'Two Dublin vestals . . . elderly and pious, have lived fifty and fiftythree years in Fumbally's lane. . . . They want to see the views of Dublin from the top of Nelson's pillar. They save up three and tenpence in a red tin letterbox moneybox. . . .' Stephen's savage indignation is an ennoblement of Crawford's meaningless rage. At the top of the pillar comes the apposite climax: the two old women, not breathless with rapture but just out of breath, settle down on their striped petticoats to eat their plums and spit out the stones through the railings as they look up at the statue of – the onehandled adulterer.

Asked the title, Stephen makes his meaning explicit: '*A Pisgah Sight of Palestine or the Parable of the Plums*'. His un-Mosaic view of Palestine, here denoting Ireland, is like Bloom's dismal view of that country in the *Calypso* episode as 'A barren land, bare waste.' The Promised Land, and the ancestral figures who lead to it, religious-combative like Moses, secular-combative like Nelson, have hardened on their pedestals. For in life, if stonehearted Moses was 'a man supple in combat', bronzehearted Nelson was a man supple in love ('Tickled the old ones too', the editor comments). Both peoples, paying lipservice to shibboleths, remain in bondage, both heroes have turned to statues. Stephen thinks in a later chapter: 'They are still. Once quick in the brains of men. Still: but the itch of death is in them, to tell me in my ear a maudlin tale, urge me to wreak their will.' In *A Portrait* he had dreamed of a long curving gallery, like the saint-studded gallery at Clongowes: 'From the floor ascend pillars of dark vapours. It is peopled by the images of fabulous kings, set in stone. Their hands are folded upon their knees in token of weariness and their eyes are darkened for the errors of men go up before them for ever as dark vapours.' These kingly gods require a submission which Stephen will not accord. Nor will Bloom, whose attitude towards stone is suggested by his visit to the museum to find out whether Greek sculptors have carved anuses on the goddesses. Both men use life as their standard of measurement.

The episode proceeds by magnification and parvification: Brayden and Walsh, Moses and Nelson are elevated to monumentality, then abruptly brought down. The alternation suggests a method which is employed throughout the chapter, based upon its organ, the lungs, supported by the four-chambered heart. Respiration begins, as it should, at the start, with the two contrasting sentences:

> Grossbooted draymen rolled barrels dullthudding out of Prince's stores and bumped them up on the brewery float. On the brewery float bumped dullthudding barrels rolled by grossbooted draymen out of Prince's stores. [115; 148]

The breathing can be felt in paired phrases and words as well, such as 'Scissors and paste', 'Way in. Way out', 'Thumping, thumping', 'Clank it. Clank it.' Almost everything is coupled. The trams start and stop, the doors open and close, people enter and leave, we move from office to street. When others try to fill their sails, Bloom and Stephen take the wind out of them. They also parody the lungs by their remarkable pairings of two saviours and two old women, the latter described entirely in a kind of respiratory duet. Crawford invites and refuses, encourages Bloom and then tells him that the publican Keyes can 'kiss my royal Irish arse', a nice blend of nationalism and exhalation. Bloom thinks that newspapermen are 'Hot and cold in the same breath.' Inflation and deflation find dozens of examples. The 'debagging' of the winds is assisted by various means: the repeated sound of slitting ('sllt'), the action of cutting, passing in, pushing in, slamming a doorknob against a back, flinging open, slipping words deftly into the pauses of the clanking presses. The newspaper headlines also follow a respiratory pattern, in a somewhat different way. The early ones are ballooned, grandiloquent summaries to suggest inhalation, while the later headlines exhale in an atmosphere of comic reduction, as in the reference to Nelson's lost arm as 'diminished digits' and to the two old women as 'frisky frumps'. Stuart Gilbert indicates that Joyce was comparing Victorian newspapers with modern tabloids, but the comparison takes its meaning from the pervasive rhythm of breathing. Against illusion and blasted illusion is the real creature, not only lunged but bodied and headed.

Joyce may seem unduly zealous in pursuing pulmonary take and give; he had, however, his justifications. He liked to work his prose into patterns as intricate and individualized as the initial letters in the Book of Kells, and he agreed with Ezra Pound that 'great literature is simply language charged with meaning to the utmost degree'. If, as Lionel Trilling has remarked, 'there is form in Lawrence's passion', there is passion in Joyce's form. His meaning is enforced in every word. But he had a further reason: he conceived of his entire book as a silent, unspoken portrayal of an archetypal man who would never appear and yet whose body would slowly materialize as the book progressed, linguafied as it were into life. This creature's presence can be felt distinctly here for the first time, encompassing, in his rhythm, both the invaders and defenders of the city.

The newspaper headlines introduce another complication which is to become important later. Their authorship is unclear. Is it perhaps the muse of the fourth estate – if the fourth estate has a muse – who becomes slowly infected with a lung disease? Or is it the omniscient author of traditional fiction, back now in motley instead of his old sober attire? Certainly his distortions whether of intake or outgo blatantly and ludicrously contrast with the efforts of Bloom and Stephen to undistort. By whomever composed, the headlines serve as a warning that the view of reality so far presented may not suffice indefinitely, that the world may move less reliably in later chapters than it has so far.

A Cheese Sandwich (8)

Many novelists never give their heroes a square meal. Joyce takes care that Bloom should have three. The lunch he provides for him is rather skimpy, just a glass of burgundy and a Gorgonzola sandwich, enough to tide him over from breakfast to an early supper. The menu is not chosen haphazardly; it is foreshadowed from the beginning of the luncheon episode which is known as the *Lestrygonians* – who in the *Odyssey* were cannibals. The narrative element is here slight, and the episode is generated mostly out of two different attitudes towards food and sexuality. These have some connection with Homer's talismanic topography, which situates the Lestrygonians in a harbour formed by two headlands exceedingly close to each other.

The first of the two headlands is indicated at the beginning when Bloom observes with some repugnance 'A sugarsticky girl shovelling scoopfuls of creams for a christian brother.' The spectacle leads him to imagine the 'lozenge and confit manufacturer to His Majesty the King. God. Save. Our. Sitting on his throne, sucking red jujubes white.' God and King seem in confectionary collusion. The Christian brother, as representative of the spirit, and the King, secular authority, alike gorge themselves on this oversweet food, white or red. This is the paternalistic side of authority, but it is not always so complacent. The thought of red jujubes at once connects with Bloom's next observation. A YMCA young man puts a throwaway into his hands which at first seems to say 'Bloom' but on closer inspection proves to say 'Blood' – specifically 'Blood of the Lamb'. The combination of lamblike innocence (in the YMCA young man, in Christ) and 'bloodiness' takes up the 'white jujubes red' but in a less innocuous way. The throwaway announces the impending arrival of the evangelist J. Alexander Dowie from Zion (Illinois, not the Middle East). Bloom is put in mind of the bloodthirstiness of church and state: 'Birth, hymen, martyr, war, foundation of a building, sacrifice, kidney burntoffering, druid's altars.' He finds a surprising union in what would seem two quite different persuasions, that of the missionary and that of the cannibal: they share a relish for blood.

The lowliness of food does not diminish its value as an index of character. Bloom's thoughts always begin close to the ground, as Stephen's all begin in air. Stephen's spiritual remorse, his backbiting of conscience, is balanced by Bloom's disgust. In the one the mind is brought to the point of vomit, in the other the stomach. Throughout this episode Bloom is hungry for lunch and yet in peril of being put off his food. He observes the Dedalus daughters, victims of malnutrition, and he considers examples of perverse gormandizing, such as rats drinking and vomiting in brewery vats. He throws some Banbury cakes to the seagulls but their rapacity makes him remember how they spread foot and mouth disease. This in turn makes him think of venereal disease, a genital discharge which for a dreadful moment Bloom imagines Boylan's vomiting into Molly. Boylan is an example of malign fleshliness throughout the chapter, and at the end of it makes his unwanted appearance in person.

Besides venereal diseases there are mental ones, and Bloom now meets Mrs Breen. He learns of the postcard her husband has received, on which 'U.P.: up' has been written by some malicious hand. Breen's madness is the vomit of mind, but the postcard, which implies that in erection he emits urine rather than sperm, suggests another organ of vomit, and brings the processes of generation and corruption as close as Bruno could have imagined. From Mrs Breen Bloom also learns of Mrs Purefoy, who in three days of labour has failed to vomit her baby from her womb. The relation of indigestion to birth is continued in Bloom's thoughts as he considers how excessive progeny eat their parents out of house and home.

The antithesis of cream and blood is reasserted in the fleshliness and fleshlessness of the people Bloom meets: Breen is fleshly, the other madman, Farrell, with his many Christian names, moving with great purposefulness around lamp-posts, seems fleshless. (Joyce avoids saying, in this episode dominated by the moon, that Farrell was familiarly known in Dublin as 'Endymion', but he does present two kinds of lunatic.) A sterner contrast is that between two other driven men, George Russell on the one hand and Blazes Boylan on the other. Bloom overhears Russell in conversation with a young poet named Lizzie Twigg. Russell is descanting mystically 'Of the twoheaded octopus, one of whose heads is the head upon which the ends of the world have forgotten to come while the other speaks with a Scotch accent.' Joyce parodies here Walter Pater's description of the *Mona Lisa* as 'the head upon which all "the ends of the world are come" '. But he is mostly concerned with the absurd innocence of Russell, in not perceiving the incongruous sexual connotation of his words, and in so overvaluing head over body that he endows his mystical octopus with two heads – a nauseating image. It is related to the sticky innocence of the Christian brother eating candy creams, and to the lamblike aspect of religion.

Bloom comments to himself on what he hears Russell saying: 'Something occult: symbolism. Holding forth. She is taking it all in. Not saying a word.' Holding forth and taking it all in are parodies of sexuality, the more so because the relations of Russell and Miss Twigg are so obviously ethereal. The unreality of Russell's conversation is heightened for Bloom when he notices from what restaurant they are emerging: 'Coming from the vegetarian. Only weggebobbles and fruit. Don't eat a beefsteak. If you do the eyes of that cow will pursue you through all eternity. They say it's healthier. Wind and watery though. Tried it. Keep you on the run all day.' The denial of fleshliness is part of that otherworldliness which Bloom sums up as insipid:

> Her stockings are loose over her ankles. I detest that: so tasteless. Those literary ethereal people they are all. Dreamy, cloudy, symbolistic. Esthetes they are. I wouldn't be surprised if it was that kind of food you see produces the like waves of the brain the poetical. For example one of those policemen sweating Irish stew into their shirts; you couldn't squeeze a line of poetry out of him. Don't know what poetry is even. [163; 210]

He is now to experience the lopsided opposite of otherworldliness. But first, on the way to the Burton restaurant, he meditates on his married life, on Molly's understanding with Boylan, reached twelve days before, on Martha Clifford's letter, on a possible return home to interrupt his wife and her lover. Just as earlier 'Kidneys were in his mind', so now, to his morose delectation, 'A warm human plumpness settled down on his brain'. Martha's question about Molly's perfume leads to the sentence on which Joyce said he laboured for hours, 'Perfume of embraces all him assailed. With hungered flesh obscurely, he mutely craved to adore.' His palate seasoned by sensuality Bloom enters the restaurant, only to be rudely jarred by the sight of men crowding the counter, 'wolfing gobfuls of sloppy food', spitting halfmasticated gristle back on to the plate. The sight is as nauseating as the idea of an octopus with two heads. Bloom cannot bear it. He says in loathing, 'Eat or be eaten. Kill! Kill!' This is Bloom's dark night of the body. For a moment he considers vegetarianism as a better recourse, but the thought of stinking garlic puts him off. The two poles of this chapter, one white and one red, one fleshless and the other flesh-and-bloody, are now energized, and Bloom is forced to make an existential choice or go without his lunch.

In this jesuitical crisis he enters Davy Byrne's pub. First he orders a glass of burgundy, vegetable in origin but quite altered from its original. But the main decision is still to come. He is tempted a little by sardines, and remembers his childhood nickname of 'Mackerel'; fish can survive in water as neither meat-eating nor vegetable-eating landlubbers can. But he hits on a better choice, a cheese sandwich, because cheese is neither vegetable nor meat: it is formed from mammal's milk without slaughter, and enclosed in bread which is vegetable in origin but reconstructed by man.

He is not to eat this temperate food unchallenged. Nosey Flynn asks about the concert tour, 'Who's getting it up?', a question offensive to Bloom both in its verb and in the answer it requires. He is evasive, but Flynn asks directly, 'Who is this was telling me? Isn't Blazes Boylan mixed up in it?' Bloom's response is measured in gustatory terms: 'A warm shock of air heat of mustard haunched on Mr Bloom's heart.' He manages to concede the point, and Flynn remarks, 'Blazes is a hairy chap.' Hairy means clever but it is an adjective suited to Lestrygonians, whose sexuality is a kind of primitive cannibalizing of woman's flesh.

Bloom has another weapon against the Lestrygonians, whichever food they devour, and that is memory. Joyce in

his melancholy moods regretted not having more imagination, but in a sanguine moment remarked to his friend Frank
Budgen that 'imagination was memory'. Bloom's mind now
presents a delicious recollection of young love. The sexual
appetite has the same fastidiousness or vulgarity as the
stomachic one, and is equally a contest between satisfaction
and indigestion. So this memory of Bloom's is particularly
risky, involving as it does both sexuality and food. The risk
begins as he watches two flies buzzing on the window pane,
'stuck' together – an image of carnality as sickening as the
sticky creams being purchased by the Christian brother.

Joyce probably has in mind Flaubert's description of Emma
Bovary as she was when her future husband first saw her,
with flies drinking from the wine glass by her hand. But what
Bloom remembers, as what Charles Bovary perceives, is
beyond the flies, who frame and contrast the human scene:

Glowing wine on his palate lingered swallowed. . . . Seems
to a secret touch telling me memory. Touched his sense
moistened remembered. Hidden under wild ferns on Howth.
Below us bay sleeping sky. No sound. The sky. The bay
purple by the Lion's head. Green by Drumleck. Yellow-
green towards Sutton. Fields of undersea, the lines faint
brown in grass, buried cities. Pillowed on my coat she had
her hair, earwigs in the heather scrub my hand under her
nape, you'll toss me all. O wonder! Coolsoft with ointments
her hand touched me, caressed: her eyes upon me did not
turn away. Ravished over her I lay, full lips full open,
kissed her mouth. Yum. Softly she gave me in my mouth
the seedcake warm and chewed. Mawkish pulp her mouth
had mumbled sweet and sour with spittle. Joy: I ate it: joy.
Young life her lips that gave me pouting. Soft, warm, sticky
gumjelly lips. Flowers her eyes were, take me, willing eyes.

Pebbles fell. She lay still. A goat. No-one. High on Ben Howth rhododendrons a nannygoat walking surefooted, dropping currants. Screened under ferns she laughed warm-folded. Wildly I lay on her, kissed her; eyes, her lips, her stretched neck, beating, woman's breasts full in her blouse of nun's veiling, fat nipples upright. Hot I tongued her. She kissed me. I was kissed. All yielding she tossed my hair. Kissed, she kissed me.

Me. And me now.

Stuck, the flies buzzed. [173–4; 223–4]

A seedcake full of spittle, passed from mouth to mouth, might be revolting; what saves it is Bloom's attitude. Food is tinged with feeling, and food and sex attain an exquisite blend in a cake made of seeds. Until this point it was sensitivity which enabled Bloom to avoid the Lestrygonian coarseness and its cloying opposite, blood and cream, meat and vegetable, gross fleshiness and crass fleshlessness. But greater than fastidiousness is affection. Love animates his imaginative memory and allows him to bring forth a succulent tidbit from his mental larder.

Fortified by this imaginative repast as much as by his Gorgonzola sandwich, Bloom leaves the pub, only to catch sight of the Lestrygonian Boylan. To avoid meeting him Bloom quickens his pace, his heart – both physical organ and seat of the affections – greatly agitated. He looks everywhere but at the approaching figure, goes through his pockets as if searching for something, and casts his eyes on the buildings he is passing as if to appraise their architecture. His eyes take in 'cream curves of stone'. Immediately after he turns aside through the museum gate and is safe. 'Cream curves of stone' is a final shot at Boylan, who because of his lack of feeling turns supple women into feelingless objects. Womanizing is like gormandizing. While love animates its object, mere fleshiness petrifies it.

The Riddle of Scylla and Charybdis (9)

Having helped Bloom to swim unscathed between fauna and flora in the *Lestrygonians* episode, Joyce had now to enable Stephen in *Scylla and Charybdis* to fly. This episode, being the ninth, concluded the first half of his book, as *Penelope* was to conclude the second half. Its importance is attested by its position, and borne out by Joyce's indication in his schemas that its organ is the brain and its art literature. Stephen propounds a theory of *Hamlet*, but behind his words, as I shall propose, is something else.

For this episode Joyce drew upon thirteen lectures he gave in Trieste in 1912–13, all devoted to *Hamlet*. As a young man, like Shaw and others, he had been severe with Shakespeare's dramaturgy, preferring Ibsen's, and his brother indicates that Joyce complained in Trieste of the undramatic quality of various aspects of the play, such as the redundancy that Ophelia, as well as Hamlet, should be mad. But in this episode Stephen allows himself only one criticism, that the soliloquy about the afterlife is undramatic and improbable. (He utters a single complaint also against another maker, God, for creating light on the first day and the sun and moon two days later.) Joyce was clearly fascinated by Shakespeare, even if he could not write like Ibsen. (Nora Joyce is reported to have said, 'There's only one man he has to beat now, and that's that Shakespeare.') Her husband followed with the keenest interest the discoveries in the Public Record Office made by Charles William Wallace, published in 1910 and later, which demonstrated that Shakespeare had lived in Silver Street with a Huguenot, and which documented his business acumen.

Joyce had also read the recent biographies or quasi-biographies by Dowden, Lee, Harris, Wilde, and Brandes. Most of these took Hamlet for the author's self-portrait. But this was like suggesting that Joyce was to be identified only with Stephen Dedalus. If Shakespeare was to write like God the folio of this world, he must be more than Hamlet. First Stephen has to display the inadequacy of other interpretations of Shakespeare's play. One such is Goethe's, that Shakespeare was a 'beautiful ineffectual dreamer who comes to grief against hard facts', and another is George Russell's, which maintains that Shakespeare is spiritual depth upon depth, a vortex of soul, an oracle for 'formless spiritual essences'. Against these Stephen insists that Shakespeare was no mollycoddle, and that his art depended as much upon hard facts as upon soft imaginings. To Russell the individual may be a soul trapped in its fleshcase, to Stephen it has an Aristotelian identity. The occultists would have it that 'This verily is that. I am the fire upon the altar. I am the sacrificial butter', but Stephen counters, 'One hat is one hat.' He anchors Shakespeare in time and place, and incurs Russell's scolding for 'this prying into the family life of a great man . . . the poet's drinking, the poet's debts'. Stephen inwardly retorts by listing his own debts, including one of two pounds to Russell ('A.E.I.O.U.'); he takes responsibility for his actions in this world, and does not plead either that they don't matter, being only corporeal, or that, because the molecules in his body have all changed since the debts were contracted, they were contracted by someone else.

The arrival of Mulligan makes the episode turn. He regards

spiritual realities such as the ghost as meaningless. No essences for him, erections rather. Against Mallarmé's sensitive image of Hamlet 'reading the book of himself', Mulligan offers his own play, 'Everyman His Own Wife', in which the hero abuses himself. For Stephen, Mulligan's indifference to the soul is akin to Russell's magnificent aversion to the body, and he joins these two adversaries together by a telegram, sent earlier, but now read aloud by Mulligan: 'The sentimentalist is he who would enjoy without incurring the immense debtorship for a thing done.' (It is a quotation, acknowledged later, from Meredith's *The Ordeal of Richard Feverel*.) Stephen is adroitly combining the two enemies of men's reason which contended in the previous episode, rarefaction and brutalization. The two seeming contraries share sentimentality, because both are divorced from context, neither being willing to recognize the other. They nonetheless attract each other, as is demonstrated by Russell's invitation to Mulligan, rather than to Stephen, to come to his house. Moreover, Mulligan likes to shunt between idealism and materialism: he vaunts Aphrodite as 'The Greek mouth that has never been twisted in prayer', but is less Hellenic when he alleges that Bloom is 'Greeker than the Greeks', that is, a homosexual. For Mulligan things done are inconsequential, for Russell things done are illusory, so in a way neither may be said to do anything. Stephen, however, admonishes himself, 'Do and do. Thing done', and later, 'Do. But do. Be done to', 'Act. Be acted on.' And he remarks of Shakespeare, 'He acts and is acted on.'

Joyce might have had Stephen in his theory of *Hamlet* walk a tightrope between these two extremes of body and soul, but he has in mind another way of meeting the peril of Scylla and Charybdis. Stephen attempts a synthesis, he holds that

Shakespeare's internal life as artist and external life as man in the world interpenetrated, so that his art quite literally held the mirror up to nature, that is, to the events through which he had lived. By this view Shakespeare was profoundly affected by his own situation as inadequate lover and betrayed husband, yet was able in his art to weave and unweave this image as nature wove and unwove his body. He is Penelope the weaver as well as Ulysses the doer, and this fusion of U. and P., worded as 'up', lends an additional significance to Breen's postcard in the previous chapter. As for the events that happened to Shakespeare, they were in some manner projections of his image, for he was like Socrates going forth from his house to meet what was not himself, but always meeting himself. Stephen is propounding here not subjectivism, but Vico's notion that the human world is made by man, and that we can only encounter in it what is already implicit in ourselves. Put another way, Shakespeare's plays are a record of what was possible for him, and so are his experiences. Life coexists with art as a representation of self.

The details of Stephen's theory are, as Stephen knows, barely plausible. He argues that Shakespeare is not Hamlet but Hamlet's father because Shakespeare, as actor, chose to play the royal ghost rather than the prince, and because he named his own son Hamnet. If it be granted that Shakespeare saw himself in the dead king rather than the live son, he must have regarded Anne Hathaway as the guilty queen. Stephen is even willing to name the co-respondents, and asserts that their names are discoverable among Shakespeare's three worst villains, Iago, Edmund, and Richard. Iago goes unexplained, but Edmund and Richard were the names of two of Shakespeare's three brothers. Anne Hathaway must have committed incestuous adultery with Edmund and Richard Shakespeare, as another Anne did with Richard III. If it be objected that the names were already in Shakespeare's sources, then why did he not choose other sources, other situations?

Stephen has an explanation also for Shakespeare's failure with the dark lady of the Sonnets. In the courtship of Anne Hathaway, it was she, being several years older, like the middle-aged goddess in *Venus and Adonis*, who took the initiative. Consequently Shakespeare had little confidence in himself as lover, and, when his wife took his brothers into her bed, he had less. His best friend, deputed to help him with the dark lady, betrayed him with her, and the two rages, against wife and mistress, commingled as Stephen says in a whirlpool and generated the fury of the tragedies. The reason his later plays breathed the spirit of reconciliation is because of the birth of a granddaughter.

Stephen's theory makes life and art so instantly interchangeable, and at the same time has so few facts on which to depend, that it is no wonder his hearers withhold assent. Not only does he gloss over Iago, whose name makes no sense in his automatic-conversion table, but he ignores another Richard in Shakespeare who is not villainous, and refuses to allow Shakespeare the right which Joyce himself exercised with Gogarty, of changing his villain's name. Asked whether he believes his own theory, Stephen promptly says no. He can disavow belief so easily because what he is offering here is not, as it seems, a biography of Shakespeare at all; it is rather a parable of art. The relation of experience and the language which recasts it may be subtle, yet it abides. Art is not simply the decking out in fine feathers of brutish appetites, nor is it only the use of bodies as conveniences for the channelling of deep thoughts.

The full significance of Scylla and Charybdis now emerges, without being ever quite stated. Odysseus was advised by Circe to pass close to the rock of Scylla, rather than to the whirlpool of Charybdis. As it happened, he had to pass through twice: the first time Scylla seized six of his men, but the ship slipped by; the second time the ship was driven into Charybdis, and only Odysseus survived. He saved himself by clinging above the whirlpool to the fig tree – symbolic perch. Joyce perceived that protuberant Scylla with six heads might be regarded as male (whatever sex Homer conferred), and omnisorbian Charybdis as female, and that the two might be induced to join, to become not two monsters but one – the beast with two backs. If he needed a precedent, he could find one in Dante's *Purgatorio*, where Christ appears incongruously as a griffin, half eagle and half lion.

In loftier terms, the hard facts of experience might unite with what Stephen called in *A Portrait* 'the virgin womb of the imagination' to make the word flesh. The pursuit of the ideal by Russell, or of the all-too-real by Mulligan, is wrong because it isolates. Solid earth must be transfused with liquid soul, here-and-now with timeless-placelessness. The way to escape the dangers of Scylla and Charybdis is to mate them.

The sexual act is the essential act of artistic as of natural creation. This act has to occur within the artist's brain, so that he is mother as well as father of the issuing word. Shakespeare has, therefore, like all artists, a double nature, is like Bloom a womanly man, is victim as well as victimizer, or as Stephen says, finding a use for Iago at last, 'he is the hornmad Iago willing that the moor in him shall suffer'. God himself must be both father and mother to Christ in the same way. In short the artist, combining both parents in himself, is an androgyne. In this two-backed beast are united the various symbols of maleness and femaleness in this episode – ashplant and hat, flag and pit, Prospero's buried staff and drowned book, and also the categories of time and space (joined more precariously in *Proteus*), the present and the possible, the now-here and the there-then, Stratford and London, Dublin and Paris, land and sea. What seems to set off the creative process is a deflowering, a brutalization of the soul by experience, experience which in some sense must be wished for. The brain like the body can be violated, but ultimately sees itself as ravished and ravisher.

Mulligan mocks this 'conception' by saying that he is himself his own father, and by offering to parturiate. He also offers his own play, an anti-*Hamlet*, in which he says his hero is his own wife. Instead of being androgynous, like the true artist, he is only masturbatory, like the false artist. (Yet he derides masturbation too in his parody of Yeats's love poem, 'Baile and Ailinn'.) Mulligan is all penis while Russell is all vagina. True art is copulative.

Joyce had been preparing this theory since 1903, when in his Paris notebook for 27 March he quoted Aristotle, *e tekhne mimeitai ten physin*, and asserted, 'This phrase is falsely rendered as "Art is an imitation of Nature". Aristotle does not here define art; he says only, "Art imitates Nature" and means that the artistic process is like the natural process.' He transcribed this observation into *Stephen Hero*, and added that 'In all his [Stephen's] talk about artistic perfection it was impossible to detect an artificial accent.' The theory is developed further in *A Portrait* in terms of 'artistic conception, artistic gestation and artistic reproduction'. There too the imagination of the male artist is described as female, Stephen awakens from an initiatory dream as an artist to feel his soul 'all dewy wet'; 'Gabriel the seraph had come to the virgin's chamber.' But while Joyce implied the artist's androgyny, he did not develop it with the parabolic intensity of his presentation in *Ulysses*.

Having consummated the marriage of Scylla and Charybdis, Stephen has the right to feel that he has overcome the danger which they represented so long as they were separated. Early in the episode he had regarded himself as a lapwing, a fallen Icarus, but at the end, as an artist, he throws off sonhood and becomes his own father, as Joyce may be said to have done with Stephen. At this stage he remembers his dream of having flown (he is bird to Bloom's fish), and it seems that he is now Daedalus *père*, successful airman, rather than Icarus *fils*. Joyce wrote in the Linati schema that with this episode the phase of anti-wings and the umbilicus was over. Stephen is now fully grown. After his flight, the dream led him to a street of harlots. He is recapitulating the stages of the artist's life envisaged by *A Portrait*, 'To live, to err, to fall, to triumph, to recreate life out of life.' He declines to combat Mulligan further, since Mulligan can only symbolize an aspect of his experience, just as Christ envisaged his betrayal by Judas, and Socrates by the nationalists of that age, 'the archons of Sinn Fein'. Anyway, as Circe told Odysseus, 'Flight is better than fight.' And yet, face to face with Mulligan, he feels his original hostility, and Bloom at this point passes between them, beyond their quarrel like the bird that preceded the *Argo* between the clashing rocks. As Stephen emerges he sees no birds – none are needed: the augury has been fulfilled already. The calm is post-coital. Instead two plumes of smoke mount from earth to heaven, like two reconcilers of the warring worlds. Like the two keys in *Aeolus*, they are Bloom and Stephen. God the creator has fused with man the creator, both androgynous, ostlers and butchers, Iagos and Othellos, both producing, by intercourse of contraries, life from death, generation from corruption, art from dialectic. The son without a body, as Joyce described Stephen in the first three episodes, has at the end of nine himself become capable of fatherhood. Stephen has solved the riddle of Scylla and Charybdis as Oedipus solved the riddle propounded by another double-natured creature. The answer to the sphinx's riddle was man, the answer to Scylla-Charybdis's is the act of love.

V

The Void Opens

The first half of the book culminated in Stephen's *summa aesthetica*, the synthesis of his youthful attempts to convert Christianity from a dogma to a system of metaphors. This possibility had been glimpsed before him, notably by Oscar Wilde, who remarked to André Gide that nothing in Christianity would fail to make perfect sense if transferred to the sphere of art. But no one before Stephen had explored the resultant paradoxes so extremely, or so responsibly. His *summa* brought together his seemingly disparate thoughts about putative fathers and ghostly mothers, as well as the mockeries of both by Mulligan. The true parents of the artist are less his real father and mother, who engender his body, than a ghostly pair who, in the spiritual womb of mankind, husband and wive to form the soul. Put another way, male and female elements – world without and world within, agent and reagent – copulate to form by spirit from what once was flesh the word which is fleshed spirit.

With this formulation by Stephen, Joyce arrived at a third level of the earthly comedy, reaching beyond its narrative and ethical levels yet including them. The whole book must be the proof that art can achieve the post-creation. As theory it was already exalting; to demonstrate it, it must be tested in what Dostoevsky called 'the crucible of doubt'. The next triad of chapters begins with the *Wandering Rocks*, the labyrinth of experience into which, having completed gestation, the theory must enter. Before the onslaught of intricate fact, certainty is not easily maintained. Stephen's confidence in the Aristotelian signatures of all things, in their separate identities and individual marriages of form and matter, is brayed in the mortar. What if the signatures are palimpsests, or even forgeries? What if things should be convertible to persons, like M'Intosh or 'Father' ocean? What if old reliable space and time should prove treacherous and undependable, and the universe they once supported so sturdily prove to be what Pope once thought of calling 'a mighty maze, a maze without a plan'?

At this moment when the environment's hostility becomes apparent – Joyce said in the Linati schema that the meaning of the episode was 'The hostile environment' – it is three o'clock, the hour of crucifixion. The world, as Emerson in another context announced, 'lies broken and in heaps', in eighteen little heaps and a coda, to be precise; the number of this episode's parts duplicates the total number of episodes in *Ulysses*, like a distorting mirror-image, to challenge the book's order. Dublin asserts itself as micropolis, with petty debts, petty spies, petty rebellions, petty lives and deaths, as if to deny the artist's effort to make it into Bloomusalem. Against the insistent claim of significance in the first half of the book, insignificance offers itself as the true temper of life. Joyce said the episode was conceived as 'a moving labyrinth between two banks' of the Liffey. The analogy was to the clashing and floating rocks in the Bosphorus, separating Asia from Europe, between which Jason's *Argo* had to sail. For this episode Joyce cavalierly neglected the *Odyssey*, where the adventure of the wandering rocks is avoided in favour of the Scylla-Charybdis adventure, and followed instead the *Argonautica* of Apollonius of Rhodes. Apollonius describes two mighty rocks in 'the swirling undercurrent'

(Joyce's 'roaring worlds'); Joyce has not only these two, but a series of smaller stones as well (his schema gives 'groups of citizens' as the equivalent of the Symplegades). Up to now, *Ulysses* like the true church had seemed to be founded on a rock, but what if the rock should prove to be as unmoored as those encountered by Jason, or as that of St Peter in Stephen's voyage through experience?

The vicious intromission of an uncertainty principle amid fixities and definites had been dimly heralded earlier. The madnesses of Deasy, Lyons, Breen, Farrell, and other characters in the middle episodes of each triad prevented complacency. Nightmares – personal and historical – shook the firmness of daytime. In *Aeolus* the narrative framework was agitated by the strange, unexplained headlines, which seemed almost composed by another author for purposes at variance with Joyce's. Stephen's disbelief in received religion had been multiplied by his disbelief in his newly compounded theory of Shakespeare's life, and Bloom's dubiety about enthusiasm and superstition – as the eighteenth century would have termed them – had many examples on which to operate. Although Stephen subscribed to Aristotelian certainties in *Scylla and Charybdis* as in *Proteus*, he also declared that the mind is poised upon incertitude as the world upon the void. Incertitude as a necessary and vital component of mental life was not Aristotelian, and neither was the void, a concept which Aristotle expressly denied. In Zürich, while writing *Ulysses*, Joyce said to a priest who was regaling a company under a starlit sky with the cosmological proof of the existence of God, 'What a pity that it is all based upon mutual interdestruction!' The Christian view of the heavenly spheres contented him no more than the Aristotelian.

The role of doubt in Joyce's own mental history had been

framed in *A Portrait of the Artist as a Young Man*. Stephen's
artistic convictions depend upon freeing himself from religion and nationalism. In Joyce's other books the same state of
mind appears in their heroes. Shem in *Finnegans Wake* is 'of
twosome twiminds fornenst gods' and a 'national apostate'.
In *Exiles*, Richard discovers in his wife's possible infidelity a
trial of his faith comparable to doubt for the believing Christian, and accepts doubt – as Paul Tillich would – as the air
he must breathe: 'I have wounded my soul for you – a deep
wound of doubt which can never be healed. I can never know,
never in this world. I do not wish to know or to believe. I do
not care. It is not in the darkness of belief that I desire you.
But in restless living wounding doubt.' This willing acceptance
of doubt makes it functional: doubt keeps alive in the light,
while belief is dead in the dark. Doubt may be taken as an
aspect of Stephen's insistence that man must fall because (as
he said in *A Portrait*) only through error (a word he substitutes for sin) can one become fully human and achieve
liberation in life or art. Not innocence but knowledge is the
releasing agent.

It would then follow that Aristotle is a much less active
presence in the episodes beginning with the *Wandering Rocks*
than in their predecessors. I would suggest that there is a new
philosophical presence, and that this can probably be identified as David Hume. The external evidence for this is the lecture on Blake that Joyce gave in Trieste in March 1912. It is
his only formal statement on philosophy after his early youth.
He said in defence of Blake,

If we must accuse of madness every great genius who does
not believe in the hurried materialism now in vogue with
the happy fatuousness of a recent college graduate in the

exact sciences, little remains for art and universal philosophy. Such a slaughter of the innocents would take in a large part of the peripatetic system, all medieval metaphysics, a whole branch of the immense symmetrical edifice constructed by the Angelic Doctor, St Thomas Aquinas, Berkeley's idealism, and (what a combination) the scepticism that ends with Hume.

The vision of philosophy as beginning with Aristotle and ending with Hume is not unprecedented, but it indicates that Joyce, in an encyclopedic work intended to take in the history of philosophy, religion, and literature, as well as western history, would have given prominence to Hume as Aristotle's counterpart. Joyce's notes preliminary to *Exiles*, composed about November 1913, indicate a fellow-feeling towards Hume as a Celt: 'All Celtic philosophers seem to have inclined towards incertitude or scepticism – Hume, Berkeley, Balfour, Bergson.' (The mention of Balfour, who wrote a *Defense of Philosophic Doubt* (1879), and Bergson, born in Paris of Irish-Jewish parentage, indicates that Joyce's own reading had not stopped with the philosophers of the Enlightenment.) He probably accepted a view of Hume prevalent in the nineteenth century but less popular now, as may be surmised from a question he addressed long afterwards to Samuel Beckett: 'How could Hume, an idealist, have written a history?' Beckett's answer, 'A history of representations', did not satisfy him. Joyce must have seen Hume as a mixture of sceptic and idealist, akin to Berkeley, whom Stephen describes as taking the veil of the temple out of his shovel hat.

For a sceptical philosophy, Hume was Joyce's obvious source. The unknowability of Hume's universe was an excellent contrary to the knowability of Aristotle's. Aristotle was,

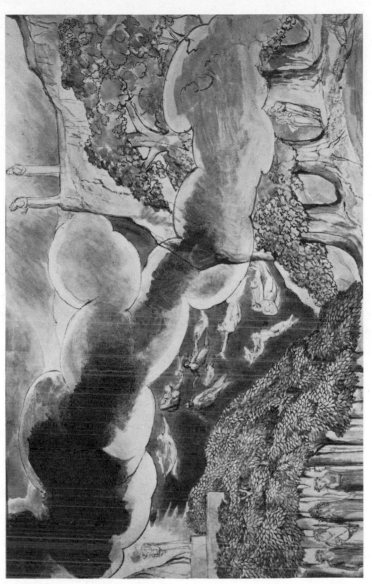

Dante and Virgil gazing
at Homer and the
Ancient Poets, from
Blake's illustrations to the
Divine Comedy, c. 1825.

Man Ray, *Imaginary Portrait of the Marquis de Sade.*

Leopold von Sacher-Masoch and Some of His Works, a cartoon from the *Wiener-Figaro* of 1875.

T. Holloway, *Hume Shaking Hands with Rousseau*, c. 1766.

as Dante said, and as Stephen quotes, *il maestro di color che sanno*, and Hume was the master of those who do not know. Hume is not prepared to assert, as Stephen is, that the soul is the form of forms, and instead declares that questions about the soul's essence, such as its degree of materiality, are unintelligible. Although he agrees with Aristotle, and Stephen, that memory is a source of personal identity, he insists that 'all the nice and subtle questions concerning personal identity can never possibly be decided, and are to be regarded rather as grammatical than as philosophical difficulties'. Against Stephen's theory of persons and things having each its signature, Hume refuses to concede uninterrupted identity. The very existence of the body is not, he holds, something that reason can enable one to maintain, though he handsomely allows that the sceptic must assent to it willynilly: 'Nature has not left this to his choice and has doubtless esteem'd it an affair of too great importance to be trusted to our uncertain reasonings and speculations.'

Hume concedes the usefulness of space and time, but he sometimes indicates contradictions in them and gives them a warranty less ultimate than Aristotle's. Stephen may have had Hume in mind, as much as Aristotle, in the *Proteus* episode when he tries the experiment of opening and shutting his eyes, and says to himself, 'Think distance.' Hume's similar discussion in *A Treatise of Human Nature*, I, iii, begins: 'Upon opening my eyes, and turning them to the surrounding objects, I perceive many visible bodies; and upon shutting them again, and considering the distance betwixt these bodies, I acquire the idea of extension.' He also discusses time in a way apposite here: 'As 'tis from the disposition of visible and tangible objects we receive the idea of space, so from the succession of ideas and impressions we form the idea of time, nor is it possible for time alone ever to make its appearance, or be taken notice of by the mind. . . . Five notes played on a flute give us the impression and idea of time.' Stephen gives the impression of time by a snatch of rhythm, 'Won't you come to Sandymount/Madeline the mare?' Hume's treatment of space and time differed from Aristotle in implying a tentativeness about their final authority. For Joyce in these purgatorial chapters, the more tentative the better.

Besides Hume's indication that the phenomenal world's standing was precarious, Joyce must also have welcomed his attitude towards his own scepticism. In various ways Hume repeats that while belief is impossible, we can retain a measure of it 'which is sufficient for our purpose, either in philosophy or common life'. He willingly concedes that, if reason cannot dispel these clouds of incertitude, 'nature herself suffices to that purpose, and cures me of this philosophical melancholy and delirium, either by relaxing this bent of mind, or by some avocation, and lively impression of my senses, which obliterate all these chimeras'. Nature makes his speculations 'so cold, and strain'd, and ridiculous, that I cannot find in my heart to enter into them any farther'. Like Stephen who appeals, with St Mark, 'O Lord, help my unbelief', Hume declares, 'A true sceptic will be diffident of his philosophical doubts as well as of his philosophical conviction. . . .' And he always returns to nature as a restorative, ''Tis happy, therefore, that nature breaks the force of all sceptical arguments in time. . . .' The ultimate appeal to nature is one which Joyce also keeps in reserve for his book's ending, but the dominant mood from the *Wandering Rocks* through *Circe* is scepticism, Bloom's day but also, for the nine hours from three to midnight, Hume's day.

Between Two Roaring Worlds (10)

The *Wandering Rocks* dally with what will become more violent later. The episode begins in a playful way the dislocations and upheavals of the sensory world, awaking it, as Hume woke Kant, from its 'dogmatic slumber'. The space-time nose is put out of joint by an element of almost total inconsequence, a onelegged sailor. He is introduced in the first section; in the second, a coin is flung to him by a generous white arm which turns out to belong to Molly Bloom. But in the third section it transpires that he has not yet reached Eccles street or the Blooms' house or begun to sing, 'For England home and beauty'. Sequence, and with it the natural order of things, is suddenly inapplicable. At the end of the third section Molly's arm appears again, to comfort us that all is not lost. Hume had shown the philosophical tenuousness of causality, the lack of 'necessary connexion' between causes and effects, and the connection is here suspended if not actively repudiated. Father Time misbehaves, offering not decorous succession but frisky agitation, and Mother Space cannot be kept at home, for scenes shift without warning, and spatial bits, such as John Howard Parnell's beard, appear causelessly where they are least expected or wanted. Some of the erratic juxtapositions are mildly dramatic, as when Boylan's conversation in a fruit store contains within it a glimpse of Bloom's behaviour in a distant bookstall. Joyce could have dislocated time and space much more than this, but he did enough to cast suspicion on the phenomenal world, to soften it up for a later knockdown.

For this episode, as Joyce indicates in the Gorman schema, not only is the Liffey the Bosphorus, but the European bank of the Bosphorus is represented by the viceroy and the Asiatic bank by Father Conmee. He names the blood as the bodily element pervading the episode, and its circulation is probably suggested in general by the river Liffey, but, in so far as the episode takes place on *terra infirma*, by the traversing of Dublin in two directions, the arterial journey to a charity bazaar by the viceroy, and the venal movement to an orphanage by Father Conmee. In *Aeolus* state and church had been represented in their inert aspect, as monuments, here they are shown in motion, while Bloom and Stephen, so lively there, are here at rest. The successful passage through the labyrinth is signalized, as Joyce intimated to Gilbert, by the 'Elijah' throwaway announcing the evangelist Dowie's advent; it floats like the *Argo* between the two Symplegadean banks, as between the North and South walls of the Liffey, and so out to sea. The viceroy upholds temporal power, but it is misdirected and mistimed, since he represents an occupying authority which is out of place and out of date, almost impotent in its courtly gestures. Father Conmee upholds spiritual power, but that power is at once urbane and anachronistic, hence out of place and date too. Both authorities are unloved.

Against such forces what shall prevail? Viceroy and priest are made a little absurd, subjected to the denigrations of comedy. The salutes to the viceroy at the end of the episode conclude with 'the salute of Almidano Artifoni's sturdy trousers swallowed by a closing door'. This irreverence intimates that the viceregal glory has not, in its resounding passage, escaped diminution. It is like Jason's dove which lost some of its tailfeathers when it tried to slip past the Symplegades. As to Father Conmee, his courtly dithering about 'old times in the barony', his blessing and prayer-reading suffer a sudden check: 'A flushed young man came from a gap of a hedge and after him came a young woman with wild nodding daisies in her hand. The young man raised his cap abruptly: the young woman abruptly bent and with slow care detached from her light skirt a clinging twig.' This too is an ironic salute from sensuality to spirituality. Joyce implies that libido thwarts sanctimoniousness, as contempt baffles authoritarianism.

But if the *'piccolo mondo'* of Dublin is a moving labyrinth between two banks, there must be a clue to the labyrinth, some way which will lead men, as it leads the river, between Europe and Asia, beyond continents and seas. (Joyce's symbology for the two continents, as the mind turned outward and inward, is very much like that of Yeats.) A clue may be sought in the behaviour of Bloom and Stephen, who coincidentally are involved in similar pursuits. Bloom is buying *Sweets of Sin* for Molly, Stephen is looking through abbot Peter Salanka's book of charms and invocations, specifically those intended to obtain a woman's love. The two books are of pornography and, to draw a word from another chapter, pornosophy, and have an unstated relation to each other. Both are verbal attempts to unite body and soul, one by sensual description, the other by psychic power. Lopsided or inept, maybe, they still represent fusions of what the viceroy and the father superior can only represent by halves. That Bloom is buying pornography for his wife adds an element of affection, which in Stephen's case is provided not by the unbought pornosophy but by his instant sympathy for his sister as she happens to pass. She, though famished, has spent a last penny to buy a Chardenal's primer in order to learn French. That ambition should still be manifested among the ruins of his family, from which in the name of art he has absented himself, torments Stephen. He will do nothing for her but sympathize, remorse being his correlative to Bloom's wincing uxoriousness. The clue to the labyrinth is to follow the river rather than to come aground on either bank. Quick fluvial feeling is better than riparian power.

This clue finds oblique confirmation in the many references, scattered through this episode, to Patrick Dignam. In life undistinguished, Dignam is undistinguished also in death: Ned Lambert, about to sneeze (in an Odyssean echo), refers to him as 'poor little . . . what do you call him'. The subsheriff Fanning asks, 'What Dignam was that?' and though many identifying signs are produced cannot remember him. But Dignam's son remembers his father well, and his portrait – which comes just before the coda – of a rather inferior father is somehow more moving than the portrait of a father superior which comes after it:

> Pa was inside it and ma crying in the parlour and uncle Barney telling the men how to get it round the bend. A big coffin it was, and high and heavylooking. How was that? The last night pa was boosed he was standing on the landing there bawling out for his boots to go out to Tunney's for to boose more and he looked butty and short in his shirt. Never see him again. Death, that is. Pa is dead. My father is dead. He told me to be a good son to ma. I couldn't hear the other things he said but I saw his tongue and his teeth trying to say it better. Poor pa. That was Mr Dignam, my father. I hope he is in purgatory now because he went to confession to father Conroy on Saturday night. [248; 324]

The simple affections please Joyce better than anything else. Fatherhood is better than viceregal or clerical paternalism.

Stephen elaborates the symbolism of the Symplegades

when he meditates, during the chapter, on the dynamo out-side and the heart inside: 'Throb always without you and the throb always within. Your heart you sing of. I between them. Where? Between two roaring worlds where they swirl, I.' He differs from the throwaway in that he moves deliberately rather than involuntarily between Asia and Europe. Being neither king's servant nor God's, he like 'Elijah' may ride safely. In the next chapter it will be Bloom who is compared to Elijah. The special status of Bloom and Stephen here is confirmed in that they, alone among the many people men-tioned, take no notice of either the viceroy or Father Con-mee. Neither *bondieuserie* nor lawandorder possesses them. This is a serious theme for Joyce, though enforced by comic devices. The episode affirms, by omission as much as by assertion, the personality which eludes both forms of authority and is, to use Stephen's word at the end of *A Portrait*, free.

Words Become Notes Become Words (11)

Having disturbed the solidity of the space-time continuum in the *Wandering Rocks*, Joyce proceeds with desolidification in the two subsequent episodes. This process has been antici-pated to a degree by Stephen Dedalus in *Proteus*, when he experiments by shutting his eyes so as to dwell entirely in the time world of the ear. He opens them again and establishes that the space world of the eye is still there. The *Sirens* and *Cyclops* episodes repeat this experiment in flamboyant ways. The *Sirens* is set in the ear world, the ear being female, recep-tive, a cave for sirens to sing in, the *Cyclops* primarily in the eye world, which is male, bulging, invasive. (At one point in the *Sirens*, as if to cast suspicion on these attributions of gender, the eye becomes female; in *Giacomo Joyce*, a work which belongs in the *Ulysses* ambiance, male eyes sexually penetrate female ones.) In the *Cyclops* the first word is I (the pronoun), which quickly connects with the last word in the initial sentence, eye (the noun). The *Sirens* episode begins with a series of sounds, a fragmentation of the larger fugal patterns to come, beginning with 'Bronze by gold heard the hoofirons, steelyringing'. The ear world, according to Stephen, with its ineluctable modality of the audible, is to be identified with time, and time urges its part as Bloom meditates in this episode on 'Time ever passing. Clockhands turning', and as the hour wheels past the point of four when Boylan is due to bring 'the programme' to 7 Eccles street. In the *Cyclops* the narrator begins by saying, 'I was just passing the time of day', an expression which denotes indifference to time as Bloom's expressions denote concern for it.

Turning up the sound-track of the ear world might have gone with stopping the film, the visual medium. Certainly that 'insoluble lump' of space must be altered, must be dissolved in music. But the space world is not to be dismissed out of hand, either here or in *Proteus*. Besides, Odysseus *sees* the Sirens as much as he listens to them, though their attentions are more auditory than visual. Joyce lets everybody peep, stare, look, with curiosity, desire, distaste, and melts all their actions and emotions and persons, subjects and objects, into sounds. The harmonic transformations are like those of Stevens's 'Peter Quince at the Clavier'. Everyone inspects Miss Douce and Miss Kennedy, the principal sirens of the episode, and everybody is inspected by them, but these young women scarcely exist except as musical motifs. The sounds range from the most primitive instrument, 'comb and tissuepaper', to orchestral instruments, about which Bloom has his humorous reservations: 'Brasses braying asses through uptrunks. Doublebasses, helpless, gashes in their sides. Woodwinds mooing cows. Semigrand open crocodile music hath jaws.' The subtlest instrument he identifies as 'The human voice, two tiny silky chords. Wonderful, more than all the others.' Beyond it is one last instrument, the human body: 'Play on her . . . Body of white woman, a flute alive . . . Three holes all women', Bloom thinks, and, of women, 'We are their harps.'

In the *Odyssey* the hero's power to hear the music is blended with powerlessness to act upon its stimulus. Unlike Odysseus, his sailors are empowered to act, but, with ears full of wax, cannot know what the stimulus is. The theme is inaction, recognized as such only by Odysseus. From total disengagement in the *Wandering Rocks*, Bloom is graduated here to pregnant inaction. (In the *Cyclops* he does act.) Joyce parallels the *Odyssey*, in a weird way, because Bloom alone fully understands the Sirens' song and can measure its sense and absurdity with the precision of a tuning fork. (Joyce evidently informed Gilbert that Bloom was the episode's tuning fork.) Moreover, Bloom alone hears the song of Boylan, a Siren song too, as he jingles in his jaunting car to Molly's bed. But such is the power of music that lust also becomes a refrain; Boylan is orchestrated with the rest, and to that extent participates in the general orchotomy which makes act into art. Figuratively, Bloom is lashed to the mast, incapable of vengeance or – to his later remorse – of return home. He is attached to his wife, nonplussed by this new development in their marriage, but – aware of his own clandestine longings, of her prerogatives as a separate individual, of the futility of direct resistance – disinclined to play spy or outraged husband. His being hamstrung finds sympathetic extrapolation in the piano-tuner who cannot see and the 'bothered' (deaf) waiter.

Joyce wrote to Harriet Weaver that he was representing in this episode 'the seductions of music beyond which Ulysses travels'. His own attitude to music was complicated; with a tenor voice almost as good as his father's, he had once considered a musical career. That he rejected it was probably from conviction as well as other considerations. During the later nineteenth century the claims of music were put forward with *brio*. It was generally conceived to be the supreme art. Wagner understandably said so, and Pater apophthegmatized the going sentiment by writing, 'All the arts aspire to the condition of music.' But Mallarmé argued that music had to work with relationships which words had already established, and Joyce, though a singer, put himself on the same side. For him all music aspires to the condition of language, and being brought to that condition in the *Sirens* episode, reveals itself as less than supreme. After he had completed this episode, Joyce told a friend that he no longer cared for music, having seen through all its tricks. And he was nettled when another friend, to whom he read the chapter, would not agree that his musical effects rendered tawdry those of Wagner. Such remarks, combined with his letter to Miss Weaver, confirm that Joyce intended Bloom to see through music, or hear beyond it.

But his doing so would be less creditable, and less Odyssean, if he had not first been captivated by its charms. It is, as he told Linati, a sweet cheat. This chapter was avowedly modelled on the *fuga per canonem*, with subject, counter-subject, and *divertimenti*, not to mention a hundred devices such as *stretti*. Opera is subsumed in the fugal form. The most brilliant operatic performer is Simon Dedalus, to whose singing Bloom and his dinner-companion, Richie Goulding, listen with delight:

> Through the hush of air a voice sang to them, low, not rain, not leaves in murmur, like no voice of strings of reeds or whatdoyoucallthem dulcimers, touching their still ears with words, still hearts of their each his remembered lives. Good, good to hear: sorrow from them each seemed to from both depart when first they heard. When first they saw, lost Richie, Poldy, mercy of beauty, heard from a person wouldn't expect it in the least, her first merciful lovesoft oftloved word. [269; 353]

The song comes to its climax, and for a moment its power is so great as to sweep all or almost all before it:

> It soared, a bird, it held its flight, a swift pure cry, soar silver orb it leaped serene, speeding, sustained, to come, don't spin it out too long long breath he breath long life, soaring high, high resplendent, aflame, crowned, high in the effulgence symbolistic, high, of the ethereal bosom, high, of the high vast irradiation everywhere all soaring all around about the all, the endlessnessnessness. . . [271; 355]

The sticking-points are in words like ethereal and symbolistic and high ('How's that for high?' is a question asked elsewhere), but Bloom does not formulate his objections till later. He hears also, though with less relish, the bass voice in Ben Dollard's rendering of 'The Croppy Boy':

> But wait. But hear. Chordsdark. Lugugugubrious. Low. In a cave of the dark middle earth. Embedded ore. Lump-music.

The voice of dark age, of unlove, earth's fatigue made grave approach, and painful, come from afar, from hoary mountains. . . . Croak of vast manless moonless womoonless marsh. [278; 365]

The two songs embody a contrast not only of vocal register but of theme, and out of this contrast the episode is generated. Ben Dollard had earlier set the twin themes by singing 'Love and War', a chesty endorsement of both. But '*M'appari*' (in English, 'When first I saw that form endearing') from *Martha* and 'The Croppy Boy' are more subtle manifestations of the Lydian mode and the Doric, one enshrining love of woman and the other love of country, Martha and Cathleen ni Hoolihan. Several other dialectical transpositions are made: the bronzebygold of the Sirens is ranked against the steelyringing viceregal cavalcade, and the romantic harp against the severe baton. Unlike 'Love and War', '*M'appari*' and 'The Croppy Boy' are songs of love lost and war lost. 'They went forth to battle and they always fell' applies to romantic leads as well as military pawns.

Bloom listens attentively but critically. Recovering from his admiration for the love song, he describes it as of the 'creamy dreamy' sort. Restless during 'The Croppy Boy', he begins to show impatience, 'Get out before the end. Thanks, that was heavenly.' His comment on the war song is concluded when, at the chapter's end, he observes on Robert Emmet's statue the bellicose peroration of Emmet's speech at the dock, 'When my country takes her place among the nations of the earth then and not till then let my epitaph be written. I have done', and farts. Joyce had once written from Rome to his brother that he was saving the 'breaking of wind rerewards' as his symbolic farewell to the Eternal City, and a similar symbolism sputters here. In the *Lestrygonians* episode Bloom was sensitive amid crudity, here he is crude amid operatic sentiment.

Bloom's refusal to accept the mad blandishments of either erotic or martial music is apparent in his steady insistence, comparable to Joyce's in 'The Holy Office', that 'filthy streams' be remembered in the midst of 'dreamy dreams'. Could the croppy boy really have been taken in by a soldier disguised as a priest but still wearing his yeoman cap? Bloom tests romantic patriotism by acid fact. Chamber music puts him in mind of a woman urinating in a chamber pot. Neither tenor nor bass can report the complexity of experience which he has known. Even as he listens to *Martha*, so ethereal, Bloom writes to Martha Clifford, so earthy, prudently disguising his handwriting with Greek ees (as Joyce did with Martha Fleischmann about the same time), and pretending to Richie Goulding that he is just answering an advertisement. In the midst of the 'soultransfiguring' music, Bloom holds his newspaper unfurled in front of him as a shield, and makes sure the blotter does not carry a mirror-image of his letter. He is sufficiently wooed by Martha's siren note to send her a postal order for two and six. And at the end of his note he puts a postscript which is a little siren song of his own, 'La la la ree. I feel so sad today. La ree. So lonely. Dee.' His prurience answers hers, but without the commitment of a promised meeting. Even as he yields a little to Martha, his thoughts keep returning to his real lure, which is Penelope. Later on, he thinks, he will buy Molly a present. Joyce says in the Linati schema that a character in this episode is Orpheus, and the most likely candidate is Bloom, trying to win his Eurydice back from the Lethean shadows of forgetting him.

The seduction note is carried for Bloom not only by Martha and Penelope but by the barmaid, Miss Douce – a virgin as he supposes, whom he mistakenly thinks to be interested in him, and the whore of the lane, whom he does not wish to patronize. He passes both unscathed. But the falsity of operatic love is not only detected by Bloom, it is disclosed to the reader in other ways. Virginal Miss Douce, in snapping her garter to answer the appeal of Boylan and Lenehan, 'Sonnez la cloche', indicates the complexities of virginity. She puts up a bold front, but underneath is pathetic, just as the sirens are human above the waist but dissolve in fish tails below. 'Mermaids' are here cigarettes, not types of nubility. In a similar way, Boylan points to the corporeal aspect of love by his jingling voyage, 'carracarracarra cock', to Molly. His is a 'song without words', as Bloom thinks. His response is bass because indifferent, flybynight; the romantic tenor is removed equally, by idealization, from genuine relationship.

Bloom registers the true way. As index of his freedom from both extremes, he dissociates himself from music. 'Freer in air. Music. Gets on your nerves', is his final verdict. He has already shown displeasure at people who listen to the siren songs of music too passionately, Bob Cowley for instance: 'Cowley, he stunts himself with it; kind of drunkenness. Better give way only half way the way of a man with a maid. Instance enthusiasts. All ears. Not lose a demisemiquaver. Eyes shut. Head nodding in time. Dotty. You daren't budge. Thinking strictly prohibited. Always talking shop. Fiddlefaddle about notes.' In sum, 'All a kind of attempt to talk.' Bloom rescues himself by sharp observation, by wariness of entanglements, and, like Odysseus, by a kind of semi-fidelity to his wife.

Joyce's friends who read the *Sirens* episode in manuscript were dismayed by its musical tricks. But these were introduced so that they might at last be repudiated as beguilements. Words, turned to notes, take back their own again and become words once more. Music is like the shell, which, according to Bloom, gives back the sound of the listener's ear. Ulysses recovers his verbal universe. But that universe is much shaken, not only because of the specialization which has made everything auditory, but also because of the shaken confidence in the narrator. In the *Aeolus* episode the interior monologue retained its verisimilitude, but here an unknown composer interpolates stray notes at will in Bloom's reflections, and invents an unsung song for Boylan.

When Joyce was told that the representational validity of the internal monologue had been questioned by critics, he replied, 'From my point of view, it hardly matters whether the technique is "veracious" or not; it has served me as a bridge over which to march my eighteen episodes, and once I have got my troops across, the opposing forces can, for all I care, blow the bridge sky-high.' In fact, he constantly expanded the monologue by non-representational methods, and in the *Sirens* episode he stylizes it to the point of absurdity. Fictional devices begin to break up as if they had grown sceptical of themselves. The presiding imagination of the book appears more and more distinct from his characters, with purposes to which they are only tributary.

Bloom Unbound (12)

In the *Cyclops* episode, the tampering with the surface of events is effected by means of a pair of narrators. The episode must have been difficult to write – how compose anything beyond the *Sirens*? – but Joyce manages to bring it off. Probably this episode profits from the famous scene in *Madame Bovary* where Emma and Rodolphe exchange tender sentiments about love while the judges of the cattle fair call out the prizes for pigs. Flaubert grants nature a straightforwardness against the false sentimentality of Emma and Rodolphe. Joyce in the *Cyclops* episode disproves sentimentality and swinishness both. He had already worked with inflation and deflation in the *Aeolus* episode, where Stephen's parable undercut Dublin's oratory. But that was a benign deflation; there is another kind of deflation, a malign one, which is inspired by meanness rather than by honesty. One of the two narrators of *Cyclops* – the one who carries the burden of the narrative – is a man of this kind, a man never named, but privately identified by Joyce with Thersites, the meanest-spirited man in the Greek host at Troy. It is Thersites who declares in Shakespeare's *Troilus and Cressida*, 'Lechery, lechery; still, wars and lechery.' His is a savage temperament, bent upon reduction. Joyce makes his Thersites a collector of bad and doubtful debts, an occupation which opens to him the worst secrets about everybody. That there might be a better side is inadmissible. A sponger and backbiter, he has no better side himself. He expresses more patently than Mulligan or Boylan the spirit of denial; sexless himself, he happily denies sexuality (as well as decency) to others. Much of what he claims to know is false, as his evident relish in every malicious tidbit implies. What he sees he sees vividly, but he has a blind eye.

Joyce lets Thersites lead off: 'I was just passing the time of day with old Troy of the D.M.P. at the corner of Arbour hill there and be damned but a bloody sweep came along and he near drove his gear into my eye.' Here, as Gilbert indicates, is the first of the multitudinous references to putting out eyes which punctuate this episode, and allude to Odysseus' blinding of the Cyclops with a sharpened stick. But what is equally pointed is Thersites' obsequiousness towards the D.M.P., the Dublin Mounted Police. He is a coward before authority, frightened by any breach of the law, and Joyce reminds us of this at the end by having Thersites say that the Citizen, had he succeeded in hitting Bloom with the biscuit tin, would have been lagged for assault and battery and Joe Hynes for aiding and abetting him. Thersites pretends to be an outlaw, but no one minds more sheepishly than he the tables of the law.

As counterpart to Thersites Joyce establishes a second narrator, whose interruptions are sometimes a bit dull. They are not for that reason less necessary. Thersites initiates, the other narrator seconds in a different mode. What Thersites puts baldly, the second narrator figleaves over. Joyce speaks of the technique of this episode as gigantism, no doubt thinking of the size of the Cyclops, but it is actually a give and take between belittlement and magnification. Thersites is all bile, his counterpart all oil. One is myopic, the other presbyopic. Thersites can take fairly innocent acts and make them out to be vile, his counterpart takes vile acts and makes them part of a frothy blancmange. In the Linati schema, Joyce indicates that Galatea plays a part in this episode, and it must be she, out of Handel's *Acis and Galatea*, who is wooed by Polyphemus the Cyclops but is unyielding there, as here, to his point of view. She trips while he lumbers. Perhaps also, since Joyce identifies the first narrator with Thersites, he has another narrator in mind, of an opposite disposition. His identity may be surmised: he strongly resembles Dr Pangloss, in that he glosses over what Thersites regards as the worst of all possible worlds and makes of it the best. In this triad of chapters where the presence of Hume begins to be felt, he is joined by another eighteenth-century philosopher, 'that moderate man Voltaire'.

Besides the Cyclopeans Thersites and Pangloss, whose different eyefuls make double vision the dialectic of the episode, another Cyclopean, the Citizen, is introduced. The Citizen reflects the intensities of the first two in that, as a chauvinist, everything Irish is good, everything unIrish is vile. Yet Joyce notes that the Cyclopeans were not only inimical to foreigners, but also unfriendly to each other. The Citizen is flagwaver and xenophobe, but he is also sponger and braggart, and, as Thersites attests, is not so Irish as he pretends, since he has broken the patriotic code by buying up the holding of an evicted tenant.

Joyce was delighted with the theme of the Cyclops. One-eyeism required the two one-eyed narrators and the one-eyed Citizen. In one way or another all the characters except Bloom are monocular. But Joyce was also pleased that Odysseus, asked his name by the Cyclops, replied '*Outis*' (a pun on his real name) or 'No one', as if disdaining any identity; then, to compensate, when he and his men are almost safe away from the wrathful, blinded Cyclops, the hero cried out to him his full name, including its other half, Zeus (in Joyce's etymology). With this hint of his enemy's whereabouts and true identity, the Cyclops threw the rock which almost cut short these epical adventures. Joyce could easily see that in the *Cyclops* episode he must have Bloom, nominally a Christian, avow himself to be a Jew, and do so at the expense of prudence. He must also have Thersites know that Bloom's father had changed his name by deedpoll from Virag to Bloom.

To emphasize his theme Joyce frolics a good deal with namelessness and with names, with identity and mistaken identity. Among the details with which he thickens the major elements, little Alf Bergan imagines he has seen Paddy Dignam – or, as Doran half misnames him, *Willy* Dignam – still alive. The Citizen is never named, and Bloom in large stretches of the chapter, especially beginning and end, is referred to without being named. A dark horse has won the race, and Bloom is called 'a bloody dark horse himself'. The Citizen, because of his purchase of the evicted tenant's holding, is only half the man he seems. Bloom is temporarily blinded in not knowing what has stirred up the Citizen and the rest against him. But there is in fact a steady attack upon Bloom from all directions: he is not Bloom but Virag; he is not a man; he takes to his bed at times like a menstruant woman; he is no Irishman but what Thersites calls a Jerusalem cuckoo; he is no patriot, the Citizen insists; he is no husband, being a cuckold; no father (his child must be a bastard); worst of all, from Thersites' point of view, he is no treater. These are all aspects of Odysseus as *outis*, attempts to make him embody no-ness.

As a result of the hostility to Jews which Thersites manifests from the first page of his narrative, and of Bloom's assertion of himself in argument, as well as of the resentment at Bloom's supposed winnings on the race, he is placed in physical danger for the first time in the day. The Citizen's physical attack with the biscuit tin is the culmination of a series of lesser attacks. In *Scylla and Charybdis*, Shakespeare suffered the indignities of love; here in the *Cyclops*, Bloom must suffer the indignities of hatred. Thersites cannot abide Bloom or anything about him, his appearance, his speech, his vocabulary, his fund of information, his refusal to drink, his

generosity to the widow Dignam. Joyce presents Bloom here
as his worst enemy sees him. Not that Thersites is altogether
disrespectful; as Joyce indicated to Frank Budgen, there is a
sneaking admiration for Bloom's conversance with all subjects. Thersites is himself almost tonguetied, his only
remarks to the company being about drink.

Yet it is here that Bloom must show himself to be, on a
minuscule stage, a true hero. Joyce was alive to the danger of
falling into a little propaganda, in the way that he thought
Tolstoy's 'Master and Man' had done. Up to now Bloom has
confronted hostile forces chiefly in his mind. Now he must
meet them directly. He must be allowed to state an ethical
view which is superior to that of the people around him. It
is more Christian than Judaic, more Platonic than Aristotelian: Joyce selected what he needed. But it must not be
sentimental. Bloom has said that Ireland is his nation, but he
adds, 'And I belong to a race too . . . that is hated and persecuted. Also now. This very moment. This very instant.' The
Citizen accuses him of Zionist daydreams, 'Are you talking
about the new Jerusalem?' 'I'm talking about injustice',
Bloom replies. John Wyse Power advises, 'Stand up to it
then with force like men.' This rebuke leads Bloom to his
culmination, 'But it's no use. . . . Force, hatred, history, all
that. That's not life for men and women, insult and hatred.
And everybody knows that it's the very opposite of that that
is really life.' 'What?' asks Alf Bergan. 'Love . . . I mean the
opposite of hatred. I must go now.' To urge men to love, and
then to speak of his own departure, connects Bloom for a
moment to Christ. More naturalistically, with this position
Bloom shows himself to be a two-eyed man; he counters
directly the various exponents of single vision, the Citizen's
chauvinism, Thersites' hatred, Pangloss's illusion.

In the Linati schema Joyce indicates that the cast of
characters in this episode includes another interloper,
Prometheus. Prometheus is a stranger addition to the cast
than Galatea. It is likely that Joyce has in mind not the
Prometheus of Aeschylus but of Shelley, whom he ranked
(along with Shakespeare and Wordsworth) as one of the three
great poets in English. Shelley's Prometheus is unbound
when he retracts his curse against Jehovah, 'I wish no living
thing to suffer pain'. He abjures as Bloom does the use of
force, and Demogorgon is thereby enabled to announce as
Bloom does the reign of love, which 'folds over the world
its healing wings'.

> To defy Power, which seems omnipotent;
> To love, and bear. . . .
> This, like thy glory, Titan, is to be
> Good, great and joyous, beautiful and free;
> This is alone Life, Joy, Empire, and Victory.

It is love which saves from what Blake called 'Single vision
and Newton's sleep', and imparts double vision, perspective.
    Perspective is itself parodied at the end of the episode
when its two historians, Thersites and Pangloss, each having
stared from his own eye in magnificent disregard of the
other, combine their dictions with a sudden click: 'And they
beheld Him even Him, ben Bloom Elijah, amid clouds of
angels ascend to the glory of the brightness at an angle of
fortyfive degrees over Donohoe's in Little Green Street like
a shot off a shovel.' In terms of the book's argument, this
apotheosis flouts space just as the *Sirens* episode flouted time
and its musical articulation. 'Am I walking into eternity along
Sandymount strand?' Stephen asks in *Proteus*, and Bloom is
propelled towards eternity now. Since the apotheosis is a

comic one, it at once exalts Bloom and recalls him to purely human proportions.

Bloom's upholding of love against 'force, hatred, history, all that', dovetails with Stephen's earlier statement that 'history is a nightmare from which I am trying to awake'. To both of them history presents itself as monolithic and glowering, the encrustations of time ready to encompass the present and future. The Citizen meets the ferocity of history with an equal ferocity. Bloom meets it with a certain kindness, a certain humour (not touched on by Shelley's Demogorgon), a certain refusal to be taken in. Against the false dialectic of Thersites and Pangloss – the impulse to wrinkle and the impulse to smooth over, to belittle and to bloat, Bloom asserts a monistic decency. His defence of love, more Christian than the Christians', rouses the Cyclops's anger, but more, it awakens the whole book towards its fourth level of meaning, the anagogic one, in which 'Love's bitter mystery' is to triumph. Stephen's theory of art has prescribed for it the act of love, but it is Bloom who must disclose what love is.

VI

The Battle for Dublin

In the adventures of Ulysses from *Aeolus* to *Circe*, Joyce displays the malign coincidence of contraries. In these chapters the contraries must be resisted, so the following schema adds a pharmacopœia of antidotes.

Episode	Contraries	Coinciding by	Product	Antidote	Presiding category	Dominant symbol	Vichian parallels
(7) Aeolus	Nature-worship/Hero-worship	Lip-service	Dead noise	Naturalism	Space	Floating island, Weathercock	Age: Theocratic Language: Sacred (Greek) Wisdom: Oracular (Tables of the Law)
	God/Machine (Jehovah/Printing press)	Publication	Hot air	Art			
	Petrified law/Volatile hard facts						
	Durability/Mutability						
	Churchman/Pressman	Christlikeness	Saviours	Mario			
	Religion/Nationalism	Fervour	Cruelty	Goodwill			
	Religion/Imperialism Greece/Rome	Mutual advantage	Status quo	Social change			
	Lord Jesus/Lord Salisbury						
	Religious/secular (sculpture)	Petrifaction	Unreality	Living tissue			
	Pedestalled living men/dead men	Inflation	Windbag	PEN IS CHAMP			
	Promised Land/House of Bondage	bloomism	Empty power Jerusalem	Short-circuit Bloomusalem			
	Inflation/Deflation	Time	Illusion and blasted illusion	Man			

(10) ...ing Rocks		Carbon pomp	Living statues	Philosophy, pornosophy	Space	Forbidden books	Age: Theocratic
Heart/Dynamo Within/Without		Counterpoint	Life	Spirit		Elijah	Language: Sacred (Latin)
Presence/Absence		Displacement	Labyrinth of objects				Wisdom: Oracular-hidden (clues)
Persons/Things Memory of the dead/oblivion							
Sequence/Simultaneity		Achronicity	Labyrinth of spirit	Body			
Grandeur/squalor		Misgovernment	Snobbery and subservience	Emancipation			
Priestly father/actual father							
Precious stones/images		Disinterment from burial earth	Artifice, Art	Metaphorical conjunction			
Pornography/Pornosophy		Erotic interest	Incomplete union	Complete union			

Episode	Contraries	Coinciding by	Product	Antidote	Presiding category	Dominant symbol	Vichian parallels
(8) Lestry-gonians	Fleshliness/fleshlessness Blood/Cream Blood of the Lamb/Feast of Our Lady of Mount 'Caramel'	Disgust	Vomit	Cheese sandwich	Time	2-headed octopus 'Mackerel' (Bloom's nickname) Stream of life	Age: Aristocratic (royalty, nobility) Language: Symbolic (poetry) Wisdom: Devious (Bloom with Mrs Breen, heavy eaters, blind man)
	Cannibal/Missionary	Elective Affinity	Blood sacrifice	Stephen's bloodless sacrifice			
	Human/Avian Carnivorousness/Herbivorousness	Esurience Mastication	Piscivorousness Stomachache	Fastidiousness			
	Lunacy (sexless)/Lunacy (sexual) (Farrell and Breen)	Juxtaposition	Vomited mind				
	Womb/Mouth	Surfeit	Indigestion, Excessive progeny (eating parents out of house and home)				
	Urine/Sperm Improper food/sex	Impotence Omnivorous-ness	'U.P.: up' Disease (venereal, ventral)				
	Food/sex	Shared regurgitation of seedcake	Spittle, Joy	None needed			

	Meaning	...quence	...ngency	Time	Sien / Tuning fork	Art: Associative (airs and pretensions)
Lydian/Doric						Language: Symbolic (operatic)
Lost love/lost war						Wisdom: Devious (Bloom with Goulding and Boylan)
Love of woman (Martha)/love of country (Cathleen ni Hoolihan, *Sonnez la cloche*)/fart						
Creamy dreamy/carracarra cock						
Harp/Baton						
Sirens/Vicercy						
Mermaids (cigarettes)/Sirens (barmaids)	Temptation	Peccadilloes				
Miss Douce (virgin)/whore of the lane	Wiles	Temptation	Perspective			
Heavenly/Hellish						
Love/Unlove						
Tenor/Bass						
Effulgence symbolistic/embedded ore						
Married complaisance/Married assertiveness						
Linger/Leave						
Accept/Reject						
Chamber music/urination						
Ear (womb)/Eye (penis)	Synaesthesia	Minor gratification				
(Deaf waiter/blind piano tuner)	Defectiveness	Incapacity	Wholeness			

Episode	Contraries	Coinciding by	Product	Antidote	Presiding category	Dominant symbol	Vichian parallels
(9) Scylla and Charybdis	Experience (hard facts)/virgin imagination Scylla/Charybdis Seeing/Hearing Aristotle/Plato Rock/Void Saxon smile/Yankee yawp Maleness/Femaleness Ostler/Butcher Ravisher/Ravished Greek gods/Greek homosexuals Lust/Surrender Theatre flag/pit Prospero's buried staff/his drowned book Iago/Othello Vagina/Elemental (spirit) Emerald stone/ring of the sea Nature/Art Perverse/Ideal Conjugal love/Scortatory love Body/Image	Beast with two backs Weaving and unweaving	Art Life and Art	None needed	Space–Time	Ashplant and hat	Age: Democratic-Bourgeois Shakespeare Language: All levels Wisdom: Art loves nature *Ricorso* (7–9): Imaginative act of love

Hamlet reading book of himself					
Onanism/Occultism					
Time/Space					
Present/Possible					
Now, here/There, then					
Land/Sea					
Stratford/London					
Dublin/Paris					
Fixed self/charging selves					
Belief/Unbelief	Necessity	Incapacitating doubt	Negative Capability		
Sundering/Reconciliation					
God/Shakespeare	Creative power	First Folios			
God/Satan	Flight and Fall	Life from Death			
(12) Cyclops					
Love/Hatred	Sentimentality	Hyperbole	Conviviality Perspective	Time-Space Empty biscuit-tin	Age: Democratic Language: Vernacular
Eulogy/Denigration	One-sidedness	Blindness			
Sugar/Salt					
Ego/Egocide	Selfhood	Falsity	Love		Wisdom: Sympathetic (Love)
Galatea/Polyphemus					
Pangloss/Thersites					*Ricorso* (10–12): Apotheosis of Bloom
Heroism/Mock heroism					
Irish/English	Sado-masochism	Cruelty	Internationalism		
Everyman/Noman	Heroic assertion	Bloom			
Eliah/Bloom	Bloom				

Three Propositions

From these warring contraries the three propositions that seem to emerge are:

I. *Men who are made to embody the ideal, or who choose to do so, become statues of stone or of flesh. Paternalism — spiritual or temporal — achieves power only to decline into loveless impotence.*

Corollary: Living tissue must be generated in another fashion.

II. *Either body or soul, if angelified or animalized, is monstrous.*

Corollary: Body penetrated by soul, and soul by body, is beautiful.

III. (a) *The real or the ideal, if pursued in isolation, appals.*

Corollary: Coupled, they delight. Art is exemplum, since it occurs only when in the act of love the virgin womb of the imagination, penetrated by living matter, conceives new flesh.

(b) *Sentimentality, whether of love or hatred, is death.*

Corollary: Love and art mimic each other's natural processes.

VII

Towards Lay Sanctity

Gods of the sun and sea, Hyperion and Poseidon between them cause the shipwreck of Odysseus, one goaded by the slaying of the sacred oxen, the other by the blinding of his Cyclopean son. These divine potencies, reflected in Irish space and time, are agitated to frenzy in the penultimate triad of episodes. In *Nausicaa*, Bloom's watch proves to have stopped at 4.30, presumably the moment of his being cuckolded, as if to contradict his unspoken thought in the *Sirens*, 'Clockhands turning.' Pathetic fallacy can go no further. Boylan's act violates the temporal order, puts time out of joint, and is so symbolized. The sun as it were stands still, Hyperion *furens*. Then, in his character of tempest-tossed voyager, Bloom joins a little, and Stephen a good deal, in the disequilibrium of the drunken students in the *Oxen of the Sun* episode. Poseidon *furens* is shaking the earth. Yet each of these episodes portrays a victory over the god who is not in the ascendant: in *Nausicaa* Bloom's masturbation, and Gerty MacDowell's, as they twist eyebeams at long distance, imaginatively defy spatial separation. In the *Oxen of the Sun* an imaginative womb controls in its watery sac two millennia of history and one of literary history. Only in *Circe* do all controls, celestial or navigational, appear for a bit as if overthrown. Humankind is hard put to raft itself over the flood.

The two gods may also be configured as idealism and materialism, or as height and depth, though these attributes undergo alterations which would be surprising if the Nolan's law of coinciding contraries had not anticipated them. The vortical sea is sometimes idealistic while high places are sometimes materialistic. But whatever their divine identities, or changes of identity, the two forces are examined in turn, sentimentalized idealism in *Nausicaa*, materialistic callousness in the *Oxen of the Sun*, and both together in *Circe*.

Heroic Naughtiness (13)

After his apotheosis at the end of the *Cyclops* episode, Bloom lands in the country of Nausicaa, Phaeacia, with a squish not a thud. The shift in scene is a reminder that we are not to be put in possession of every detail of this 18-hour day; the narrative has many gaps, and the scene shifts more rapidly than in other novels. In fact, Joyce thinks himself the only shakescene in the country; he exceeds Shakespeare's incontinence in setting Bohemia on the sea coast, by making land and sea obey his chapter divisions. *Nausicaa* has a further function in examining the anagogic level of *Ulysses* which Joyce had first seriously introduced in the *Cyclops* episode; if love is 'truly life', then what love is *not* may be a necessary preliminary to demonstrating what it is. Bloom has defined it only as 'the opposite of hatred', but Dr Pangloss, or Galatea, offered in the *Cyclops* a further gloss on it:

> Love loves to love love. Nurse loves the new chemist. Constable 14A loves Mary Kelly. Gerty MacDowell loves the boy that has the bicycle. M.B. loves a fair gentleman. Li Chi Han lovey up kissy Cha Pu Chow. Jumbo, the elephant, loves Alice, the elephant. . . . You love a certain person.

And this person loves that other person because everybody loves somebody but God loves everybody. [327; 433]

From this good round endorsement of Venus Pandemos the coyness of Gerty MacDowell is a short step:

The summer evening had begun to fold the world in its mysterious embrace. Far away in the west the sun was setting and the last glow of all too fleeting day lingered lovingly on sea and strand, on the proud promontory of dear old Howth guarding as ever the waters of the bay, on the weed-grown rocks along Sandymount shore and, last but not least, on the quiet church whence there streamed forth at times upon the stillness the voice of prayer to her who is in her pure radiance a beacon ever to the stormtossed heart of man, Mary, star of the sea. [340; 449]

Her *paysage*, not *moralisé* but *sexualisé*, is topographically like the one at the beginning of *Finnegans Wake*, where 'riverrun, past Eve and Adam's, from swerve of shore to bend of bay, brings us by a commodious vicus of recirculation back to Howth Castle and Environs'. (Eve precedes Adam in the name of the church, which is really Adam and Eve's, to take account of the feminine Liffey being mentioned before the masculine Howth Castle and Environs.) In *Nausicaa* Joyce makes Howth male, as befits a promontory, the bay and shore female, and the church, whence the voice of men praying to the Virgin at times 'streamed forth', androgynous.

In *Nausicaa*, as in 'The Holy Office' written about fifteen years earlier, Joyce relates spirituality and feminine coyness. He advised Linati that the meaning of this episode was 'The Projected Mirage'. There are in fact two mirages, the shared erotic fantasy of Bloom and Gerty, and the shared spiritual fantasy of the men's retreat at the Star of the Sea Church. Gerty observes Bloom 'literally worshipping at her shrine', and the men are worshipping literally at Mary's shrine. Both Gerty and the men seek to receive an imagined body, communion being as illusional as masturbation. Mariolatry and coyness resemble each other in that the one seeks to qualify the austere three-personed maleness of the Trinity by introducing a female presence into it, while the other allows some recognition of maleness into female purity. On a different level, that of the sea, the Caffrey twins are building, and demolishing, castles in the sand, as Bloom and Gerty, and the men with the Virgin Mary, build and demolish castles in the air.

The two forms of false idealization and imperfect love entangle themselves in the fireworks. J. C. Maxwell has discovered that Joyce here recalls the fireworks scene from Jacobsen's novel, *Niels Lyhne*, where similarly a girl experiences fires of passion and pyrotechnics. Joyce does it better, however, and he also sees a possibility which Jacobsen did not, of symbolizing in one particular firework – the Roman candle – Roman Catholic religiosity and pagan phallicism at the same time.

And she saw a long Roman candle going up over the trees up, up, and, in the tense hush, they were all breathless with excitement as it went higher and higher and she had to lean back more and more to look up after it, high, high, almost out of sight [like the high note in Simon Dedalus's song from *Martha*], and her face was suffused with a divine, an entrancing blush from straining back and he could see her other things too, nainsook knickers, the fabric that caresses the skin, better than those other pettiwidths, the green, four and eleven, on account of being white and she let him and she

saw that he saw and then it went so high it went out of sight
a moment and she was trembling in every limb from being
bent so far back he had a full view high up above her knee
where no-one ever not even on the swing or wading and she
wasn't ashamed and he wasn't either to look in that immodest way like that because he couldn't resist the sight of
the wondrous revealment half offered like those skirtdancers
behaving so immodest before gentlemen looking and he kept
on looking, looking. She would fain have cried to him chok-
ingly, held out her snowy slender arms to him to come, to
feel his lips laid on her white brow the cry of a young girl's
love, a little strangled cry, wrung from her, that cry that has
rung through the ages. And then a rocket sprang and bang
shot blind and O! then the Roman candle burst and it was like
a sigh of O! and everyone cried O! O! in raptures and it
gushed out of it a stream of rain gold hair threads and they
shed and ah! they were all greeny dewy stars falling with
golden, O so lovely! O so soft, sweet, soft! [360; 477]

Vladimir Nabokov has remarked that the description of this
sexual climax becomes a kind of poetry. It does so, poetry
impregnated with Gerty's fertile imagination. And this im-
pregnation is vital to the book's third level, which is concerned with art.

When Joyce insisted that his aesthetic was not in the least
pretentious or élitist, but was based entirely upon the
naturalness of the artistic process, he did not refuse to accept
the implications. In the first place, art is a permanent component of human life. It must not, therefore, depend for its
existence upon elaborate training, and Lenehan's compliment, at the end of the ninth section of the *Wandering Rocks*,
'There's a touch of the artist about old Bloom', is based
firmly on recognition of art's pervasiveness. The artistic

faculty must be possessed by all, in greater or less degree. Gerty's respect for poetry might seem at first to be merely a subject for amusement: 'she felt that she too could write poetry if she could only express herself like that poem that appealed to her so deeply that she had copied out of the newspaper she found one evening around the potherbs. *Art thou real, my ideal?* . . . and ofttimes the beauty of poetry, so sad in its transient loveliness, had misted her eyes with silent tears that the years were slipping by for her. . . .' It has been suggested that Joyce is here mocking Samuel Butler's book, *The Authoress of the Odyssey*, and Butler's argument that Nausicaa, not Homer, wrote that book. But even if Joyce considered the notion farfetched, it had enough truth for him to entrust half of one episode to his Nausicaa's authorship. In any case Joyce was Tolstoyan, he respected simplicity, he thought simple people were not divorced from artistic capacity. Virtually all his characters recognize poetry in some form, and quote it, or use language in a recognizably literary way, as if asserting, in the turn of a phrase, an imaginative rebellion against straight subservience. Gerty is untrained, but her impulse to art is as genuine as Homer's. Joyce propounds in this episode an aesthetic theory which goes beyond Butler's: that morose delectation, a genre distinctively and universally human, is the poor man's art form. The rich man's, too.

Gerty's character should not, therefore, be read as only a parodic version of a young woman as depicted in trashy love stories. At first it seems that Joyce's description of the episode to Frank Budgen, as done in a 'nambypamby, jammy, marmalady, drawersy style with effects of incense, mariolatry, masturbation, stew and cockles, painter's palette, clichés, circumlocutions, etc.', is sufficient. But Gerty is not so self-deluded as he implies, she also has a quality he does not mention, an underlying wariness and sharpness, a disconsolate sense of the impingement of her *real* upon her *ideal*:

> Gerty MacDowell who was seated near her companions, lost in thought, gazing far away into the distance was in very truth as fair a specimen of winsome Irish girlhood as one could wish to see. She was pronounced beautiful by all who knew her though, as folks often said, she was more a Giltrap than a MacDowell. . . . Her hands were of finely veiled alabaster with tapering fingers and as white as lemon juice and queen of ointments could make them though it was not true that she used to wear kid gloves in bed or take a milk footbath either. Bertha Supple told that once to Edy Boardman, a deliberate lie, when she was black out at daggers drawn with Gerty (the girl chums had of course their little tiffs from time to time like the rest of mortals) and she told her not let on whatever she did that it was her that told her or she'd never speak to her again. [342; 452]

Into her emollient reverie come the small abrasive interventions of the baby trying to talk, the children trying to urinate, the girlfriends trying to outrival her. Beyond wariness, Joyce presents an aspect of Gerty of which she is largely ignorant, her youth. She is young, and being so, her immaturity is not contemptible, though it leads to conceptions very different from Bloom's. The world of the young, as Robert Frost indicates in 'To Earthward', is composed of honeysuckle and musk; later these cloying pleasures will not serve, and must be mixed with salt 'and burning clove'. Gerty sees things as they might be, she is full of dreams, she is convinced of her own uniqueness, 'something aloof, apart in another sphere' (as she says), and she regards Bloom, immediate object of her affections, as also unique, different from all other men. A sense of herself as paramount in the universe is inextricably connected with her youth; so is her image of life as something novel, unpredictable, sure to be marvellous.

Bloom's way is different, and the secret spring of this episode is a contrast between not only his realism and her sentimentality, but his age and her youth. (Stephen Dedalus at twenty-two is already too old for this kind of contrast.) The middle-aged substitute for the sense of uniqueness is the sense of *déjà vu*. Bloom guesses, from the wadding that she waves at him in token of farewell, that she is menstruating, and immediately ponders on the prevalence of this phenomenon. He reflects on his own appetite for someone new, as in his clandestine correspondence with Martha Clifford, and on the discomfiting fact that subsolar, and even sublunary life has nothing new to offer. He broods on the coincidence that Martha's postal address is care of Dolphin's barn, which was where he and Molly played charades sixteen years before. 'So it returns. Think you're escaping and run into yourself. Longest way round is the shortest way home. And just when he and she.' (He refers to the simultaneity, a little forced because it depended on his watch having stopped, of the sexual acts of his wife and of himself that afternoon.) His conclusion is, 'Circus horse walking in a ring.'

In sum, the young assert their uniqueness, the old their familiarity. One is all aspiration, the other all recognition. Bloom furbishes his conception of 'The same anew' – that axiom out of which *Finnegans Wake* is generated – with many examples, such as the way that Molly and Milly have the same teeth, and often menstruate at the same time. The discovery of coincidence is the middle-aged counterpart of the youthful discovery of singularity. Joyce does not invalidate either Gerty or Bloom; May and January meet as they can and must. At the end of *A Portrait* Stephen is both young-old and old-young when, in announcing his intention to encounter the reality of experience, he says, 'for the millionth time'.

Between the two ages of man and woman the episode breaks into two parts. The change is signalized not only by Bloom's mind taking over the narrative from Gerty's, but by the sudden shift in perspective as he observes the limp which she has called her 'one small shortcoming'. This limp reduces nambypambiness to pitiable self-deception, and leaves us with an increased awareness of the terrible ways in which the body fails imagination and hope. Bloom suddenly understands the scene, and with his sympathy he and Joyce return to their centre. It was deprivation which spurred Gerty, as it spurred Shakespeare, to poetry.

As for Bloom, masturbation enables him to return to his usual solicitude for other creatures. Joyce has found an aspect of masturbation which every writer on the subject, from Rousseau to Philip Roth, has missed. For the first time in literature masturbation becomes heroic. It is a way of joining ideal and real, and while simplistic or vulgar, it is not negligible. It brings Bloom back to goodwill and away from indifference. He leaves behind Narcissus drowned in the pool.

Vagitus: The Word is Born (14)

Having examined the rites of courtship, and disclosed their untidy damp residue, Joyce turned in the *Oxen of the Sun* to courtship's results. Against the vaporization of feeling he now presents its lutulence; we are down in the mud with the crocodiles, or medical students. The mirages are gone, but the earth in its abundance has not returned; instead there are only flowerless fields, deserts which reveal the sun's potency but not his generosity. Gerty's dreamy creaminess hardens to surgical callousness.

In his characters' internal monologue Joyce had provided a view of the mind's underbelly, and he does the same with the lying-in hospital. Instead of its convex side, he shows the concave one. After some vague statements about the hospital's prestige and usefulness, it becomes the place where bodies are wrenched apart, monstrous deviations from normal birth appear, mothers and babies die. The medical students treat all aspects of fertility with the same profanation as Odysseus' crew the sacred cattle. Flesh maddens them, too. They consume voraciously, in their wild talk, all taboos about the acts of generation, parturition, and dissolution. They mock babies, mothers, fathers, and so carry on the theme of denial initiated by Mulligan, exemplified by Boylan, cogently extemporized by Thersites, and spatialized with his biscuit tin by the Citizen. Bloom finds their talk revolting, but grants that through 'metempsychosis' the heartless students will eventually become the solicitous practitioners. But for the moment, their desecration outdoes Thersites' denigration. God is invoked, generally to be blasphemed, in almost every paragraph. The episode opens with fertility charms and ends with their ultimate reversal, and perversion, in a promise to diddle Almighty God.

Joyce explained, in a letter to Budgen, that the crime against the god was the sterilization of the act of coition. The students have several ways of perpetrating this, including of course contraception. The most vigorous exponent is Buck Mulligan, whose inner sterility wears the characteristic mask of an overflowing of animal spirits: he announces his readiness to fecundate any woman in the country without charge, regardless of her social status. This is the ultimate method of sterilizing the act of coition, by disengaging it altogether from love. Mulligan mocks other forms of love by postulating as the supremest object of desire 'a nice clean old man' and by saying, in the delirious finale, '*Ma mère m'a marié*'. At the moment of expressing this sentiment, he is occupied in withdrawing his company covertly from Stephen Dedalus. Leaving his friend in the lurch – a gesture opposite to Bloom's – is one of several equivalents of *coitus interruptus* mentioned in the chapter. In fact, *coitus interruptus* becomes a verbal more than a genital matter in the episode's last pages, which are made up of a series of random ejaculations, a spray of words in all directions.

The theme of desecration finds expression also in the half-parodic pastiches of English prose styles. T. S. Eliot remarked to Virginia Woolf that these showed the futility of all style, but it could be argued that they show the utility. The flaying of men's ideals is matched by the discard of one style after another; yet as each disappears, another takes its place. The medical talk strips the bodies of men and women, only to have the outraged mind reclothe them immediately. The students simplify life down to its elemental processes, yet they do so in a surprisingly intricate way, as if thought could not be denied even when its value was being minimized. Regarded in ensemble, the pastiches constitute a remarkable tribute to the literary tradition in English as the matrix out of which *Ulysses*, or any other work in this tongue, has to issue. So while they suit the theme of desecration, they also subtly discredit it.

It must be said, too, that the styles cannot be futile any more than ontogeny is futile. They represent orderly stages

of literary genesis. Joyce pointed out that they were contrasted with the headpiece and tailpiece of the episode, which
he said were two forms of opposite chaos. The headpiece is in
a highly involuted prose, latinate in vocabulary and absurdly
latinate in syntax, as hieroglyphic as in Vico's theocratic age.
It suggests the chaos of excessive order, historically in terms
of the invasion of Britain by the Romans and their imposition
of an impossible grammar upon the easygoing aborigines. The
recovery of normal order begins when Bloom appears. Then
comes the slow development of English prose over seven (or
perhaps, deferring to human gestation, nine) hundred years
from aristocratic (symbolic) language to the democratic
vernacular. Finally there comes the placental outpouring at
the end (it is the afterbirth as well as an ejaculative spray)
which is an *aggiornamento* of style into contemporary slang.
The slang is not disparaged, any more than birth is disparaged by afterbirth, but it is shown to be not yet subject to
artistic form. Its anarchy, and the fascism of the headpiece,
contrast with the fecundity of the natural order.

If the medical students are the god's apostates, his true
disciples are Bloom and Stephen, the pregnant nurse, and
Mrs Wilhelmina Purefoy, who flouts the students' sterility
by concluding her three-day labour with the birth of a son.
Joyce's scheme for the episode included minor as well as
major imitations of the birth process. One of these was the
idea, communicated in a letter to Budgen, that Bloom is the
spermatozoon, the nurse the ovum, the hospital the womb,
and Stephen the embryo. To descant upon this explanation,
the episode contains two human embryos and two quasi-
human ones. Mrs Purefoy's oncoming baby is paralleled by
the outgoing Stephen, and by the issuing word which is at
once God's word (Christ) and the artist's word (a work of

art). It is Stephen who first leaves the hospital, 'Outflings', as Joyce says, 'giving the cry', which is the vagitus, the cry of the newborn. Although Joyce does not say so, Stephen can be thought of as sired by the English language and dammed by literary tradition. At this point in the book, however, Joyce is more concerned with the fact that Stephen is first to leave as Bloom was first to enter, suggesting comically the relation of son and father. Bloom is hospitably received by the nurse, and has conversation (a meaningful term in law) with her, so to that extent she is the putative mother, though here Joyce is indulging in a gynaecological flourish rather than a serious statement. More to the point, Bloom has in mind in the episode an image of Stephen as he is now and as he was as a child, as if the process of gestation had gone on after as well as before birth, with Bloom's paternity also continuing.

Aside from such problematic anatomical linkings, the two men are connected here by other cords. One has been usurped, one cuckolded, and Stephen draws an analogy by saying, 'Bring a stranger within thy tower it will go hard but thou wilt have the second best bed.' Both are concerned about the fertility of Irish cattle and so about the foot and mouth disease then at an epidemic state. Although only Bloom evinces sympathy for Mrs Purefoy and the nurse, Stephen conspicuously fails to take part in the mockery of women in labour or pregnancy. On crucial questions they see much the same. When the students dispute over the obstetrician's choice between saving a mother or saving her baby, all except Stephen agree that the child should die and the mother live. Stephen, never one to spare mothers, insists with some irony that the baby live and the mother die. Bloom, appealed to, avoids choice but says that if *accident* should so befall as Stephen has indicated, the Church might profit by collecting both death and birth pence. Another question broached is whether Siamese twins should be surgically separated or not if one predecease the other: Stephen's verdict is, 'Let no man put asunder what God has joined.' Underlying his joke is a conviction that the natural order should have its way, while the medical students are all for dickering with it. Bloom, to prevent their worst speculative excesses, raises questions of the predetermination of sex and the reduction of infant mortality, since like Stephen he wishes to assist, not impede nature. As usual he is kinder: when Stephen declares that if a woman has once let the cat into the bag, she must let it out again or give it life to save her own, Bloom thinks to add, 'At the risk of her own.' Both take sides against unnaturalness.

Nature is primarily Bloom's concern, while Stephen espouses that process which has been shown to be natural too, in *Scylla and Charybdis* and *Nausicaa*, namely, art. On this subject Stephen expounds Blake's assertion that 'Time's ruins build eternity's mansions', with this commentary: 'Desire's wind blasts the thorntree but after it becomes from a bramblebush to be a rose upon the rood of time.' (The thorntree comes from Yeats's poem, 'Red Hanrahan's Song about Ireland', and the 'rose upon the rood of time' is most of the title of another Yeats poem.) What is in experience intolerable is decorous in art. 'In woman's womb word is made flesh but in the spirit of the maker all flesh that passes becomes the word that shall not pass away. This is the postcreation. *Omnis caro ad te veniet*.' To the artist, as to God or death, all flesh will come, and be reanimated: 'If I call them into life across the waters of Lethe will not the poor ghosts troop to my call? Who supposes it? I, Bous Stephenoumenos, bullockbefriending bard, am lord and giver of their life.' The medical student Vincent objects that this is too big a brag for someone who has not yet anything but 'a capful of light odes to call his genius father'. But it associates Stephen with the rebirth of Christ as well as with his birth (as does Mrs Purefoy's three-day labour). And it insists that art comes from experience, for Stephen as for Stephen's Shakespeare.

He also makes clear the kind of art he is endorsing. It is not of the George Russell kind: 'Vegetables, forsooth, and sterile cohabitation!' If in art, everyman *is* his own wife, the process is not parthenogenetic. Stephen considers whether the Virgin Mary had or had not carnal knowledge of God. Pedantically using German words as if in tribute to the German philosophic school, he insists: '*Entweder* transsubstantiality *oder* consubstantiality but in no case subsubstantiality.' In other words, Mary was either of divine or of human substance, but in no case was she less than substance or had she less than sexual intercourse. He will not accept 'A pregnancy without joy, . . . a birth without pangs, a body without blemish, a belly without bigness.' Art must incorporate, and excorporate, actual life.

In 'The Holy Office' Joyce described art as catharsis, but parturition is his more mature picture of it. On Bloom's entrance into the hospital the lightning had riven, and on Stephen's departure from it the thunder sounds. As when the womb opens to expel its issue, so is the 'transformation, violent and instantaneous, upon the utterance of the Word'. The Word is specifically only the name of a pub, but its utterance is natal. Stephen issues as a figure of speech for the work of art, a work of art anthropomorphosed. The analogy is complete: Mrs Purefoy has laboured and brought forth a Purefoykin, English has laboured and brought forth Stephen, and the model work of art, whose generation was described in *Scylla and Charybdis*, may now be thought of as expelled like Minerva from the brain.

Joyce wrote Miss Weaver that the *Oxen of the Sun* is the most difficult episode in an odyssey to interpret and to execute. The interpretation seems to be this: the processes of nature and art are synonymous with each other; they imitate each other's fecundity and will not be sterilized. For both of them love is a contra-contraceptive. What nature is for the body, art is for the mind. Aestheticism falsifies art by being false to nature, materialism falsifies nature by being false to mind. By nature and by art, Bloom and Stephen alone save themselves from shipwreck.

The Orc (15)

It is midnight, the soul's not the dial's. The 'tenebrosity of the interior', as it was called in the *Oxen of the Sun*, is matched by a tenebrosity of the exterior. In the morning the sunlit world was credible, but now its devotees are asleep, and those who still keep watch see its shapes – animate and inanimate – as shadows. The self is deprived of latitude and longitude, and becomes its own place, in itself making of earth a hell or a purgatory. Form and reason no longer offer their helping hands, incertitude and remorse having supplanted them. The eye confronts no ineluctable modality of the visible, only unsought images of the invisible, lusts and loathings from within claiming autonomous existence without.

The *Circe* episode awakened Joyce's most extreme methods, not less extreme for being couched in terms of the music hall or vaudeville. He found what help he could in other authors,

and interfused Circe's transmogrifying spells with the shape-
changes which occur in *Faust* on the Brocken, in St Anthony's
persecuted imagination in Flaubert's novel, in Ovid's *Meta-
morphoses*, in Dante's *Inferno*; he also evinced familiarity with
the chaotic displacements and transformations in Freud's Id.
First images, then ethics. 'Hell is the place of those who
deny', wrote Yeats, and denial is everywhere. Persons,
denied, become animals; objects, denied, become persons.
These, and denied concepts, all take their parts in a peni-
tential surrealism. Hume is outHumed. Joyce said in the
Linati schema that *Circe*'s significance was 'The Manhating
Orc', a reference not to Blake's fiery creature but to the
amphibious monster who in *Orlando Furioso* (Cantos VIII and
X) comes close to devouring Angelica. The third chapters of
all the triads include a monster, but the Orc includes in his
huge writhing mass all his predecessors, the vulturous dog
seen by Stephen on the strand, the rat at Glasnevin, Scylla
and Charybdis before Stephen solved their riddle, and the
enormous Polyphemus. (In the last chapter of the book the
Orc is succeeded by another amphibian of more human proportions, 'Boylan's tremendous big red brute of a thing'.) In
this episode the Orc has many heads.

Beyond this compounding of monsters from literature and
from his preceding chapters, Joyce based *Circe* on an inter-
change of inner and outer reality. For this process Vico's
philosophy offered a general theory, which was more useful
than Aristotle's sharp division of perceiver and perceived. To
Vico history was the actualization in time of possibilities that
could be deduced by study of the individual mind; it moved
in patterns discoverable in that mind. Croce rephrased Vico
in the sentence, 'Man creates the human world, creates it by
transforming himself into the facts of society: by thinking it

he recreates his own creations, traverses over again the paths he has already traversed, reconstructs the whole ideally, and thus knows it with full and true knowledge.' The soul translates itself into its surroundings in time and place, or, put another way, society is a book in which to read the soul, though the soul may also be read, and more easily, in itself. Stephen has alluded to this view in *Scylla and Charybdis*, though he quoted there not from Vico but from Maeterlinck's version of the Vichian idea: '*If Socrates leave his house today he will find the sage seated on his doorstep. If Judas go forth tonight it is to Judas his steps will tend*. Every life is many days, day after day. We walk through ourselves, meeting robbers, ghosts, giants, old men, young men, wives, widows, brothers-in-love. But always meeting ourselves.' Stephen develops this conception to establish that God, should he exist, must be 'all in all of us', and to confirm that Shakespeare must be the events of his life as well as all his characters and the events in theirs. In *Circe* Stephen expresses this idea again, with the implication that it has now been amply demonstrated: 'What went forth to the ends of the world to traverse not itself. God, the sun, Shakespeare, a commercial traveller, having itself traversed in reality itself, becomes that self. . . . Self which it itself was ineluctably preconditioned to become. *Ecco!*' What we are becomes what we experience, what we experience is only what we are. Thanks to Vico Joyce in *Circe* might bring the externals of the day within the mind, but might also bring the internals of the mind into outward form.

The episode is reeled out from a warring centre of contraries. The two basic ones are soul and body, which can be found reflected everywhere, in priest and king, church and state, God and Dog, blessedness and damnation, woman and man, the rosecovered womancity which opens to become the boneridden womancity, mass and black mass. Both soul and body have their purity and their impurity factions: Mrs Breen and three ladies of quality sweep in to take a high and mighty line with Bloom, though their pudicity is close to lubricity: 'I'll flog him black and blue in the public streets.' Circe, as Bella Cohen, changes from woman to man as Bloom changes from man to woman. She also encapsulates the two contraries of soul and body, for she turns herself into the nymph (in the picture above the Blooms' bed), and in this capacity proclaims that she is 'stonecold and pure', and babbles on, 'Sister Agatha. Mount Carmel, the apparitions of Knock and Lourdes. No more desire. Only the ethereal. Where dreamy creamy gull waves o'er the waters dull.' At this point Bloom's trousers' button snaps, her soulfulness being too much for it, and he announces, 'You have broken the spell. The last straw. If there were only ethereal where would you all be, postulants and novices?' The nymph is indignant, but Bloom is firm, seizing her hand, 'Fair play, madam. No pruning knife. . . . What do we lack with your barbed wire? [A nun invented barbed wire, Bloom remarked earlier.] Crucifix not thick enough?' This counterattack is so successful that the nymph changes back into Bella, who tells him, 'You'll know me the next time', and attempts no further transformations. 'Mutton dressed as lamb' is Bloom's comment. He has perceived the secret identity of sadism and masochism in sexuality as he did in religion, and is no longer intimidated. From being transformed into a woman, he becomes once more a man.

In so far as the body stands in the brothel scene for temporal power, it has two principal manifestations, one as England, the other as Ireland. England is represented by the two soldiers, Ireland by the two watch. These forces of authority understand each other and are in collusion: both are opposed to Bloom and Stephen. England is also incarnated in Edward VII, who, haloed as Joking Jesus, prates of universal peace while his soldiers abuse the Irish. Ireland is incarnate in Old Gummy Granny, who thrusts a dagger towards Stephen's hand and says, 'Remove him, acushla. At 8.35 a.m. you will be in heaven and Ireland will be free. (*She prays*) O good God, take him!' Nationalism and imperialism both claim spiritual authority for their physical cruelty. As for the redcoats, their respect for authority is shown to be as false as the authority itself is hypocritical. Private Carr, overhearing Stephen use the word 'king', shouts, 'I'll wring the neck of any fucking bastard says a word against my bleeding fucking king.'

Because Bloom and Stephen differ in degree rather than in kind from other men, and have like others aspirations both secular and spiritual, they are driven into the purgatorial extremism of this episode. Bloom, for his schemes of social improvement, is crowned King Leopold I, and, on a more spiritual plane, is called the world's greatest reformer. His messianic goals are combined in his promise of The New Bloomusalem in the Nova Hibernia of the future. Stephen, struggling on another plane, proclaims, more elliptically, salvation, through the transubstantiated bread and wine of art. (Joyce had made similar predictions at the end of his essay, 'A Portrait of the Artist', and the ensuing novel.) Both then undergo the opposite, Bloom conviction for criminality, Stephen, potential damnation for apostasy. To his mother's warning that he should beware the fires of hell, Stephen responds as directly as Bloom had to the Citizen, by crying out, 'Shite!' To say shit to one's dead mother becomes a form of heroic enterprise: '*Non serviam*', he declares.

He tries 'eagerly' to prompt her to say 'The word known to all men', but she will not be distracted from his damnation. Translating his spiritual into physical rebellion, Stephen lifts his ashplant, shouts out, '*Nothung!*', and smashes the lamp chimney. Nothung is Siegfried's sword, but it sounds also like a parallel to Odysseus' assumption of the name 'Noman'. It in turn brings about the final destruction of time and space, whose end has for some time been near: '*Time's livid final flame leaps and, in the following darkness, ruin of all space, shattered glass and toppling masonry.*' When this act was fore-shadowed at the beginning of the episode, it was said to shatter light over the world. Here the destruction-creation at the centre of the artistic process is realized. (Samuel Beckett, in his *Proust*, quotes an apposite remark of De Sanctis, 'Chi non ha la forza di uccidere la realtà non ha la forza di crearla.') The brain's womb is also a tomb; experience dies in it to be reborn like Christ beyond space or time. The process is pain-ful, like labour, or murder. Stephen points to his forehead and says, 'But in here it is I must kill the priest and the king.' But the ultimate aim of this murder is to free mankind from its graveclothes. He tries to explain this position to the uncomprehending soldiers, 'You die for your country, sup-pose. Not that I wish it for you. But I say: Let my country die for me. Up to the present it has done so. I don't want it to die. Damn death. Long live life!' In this declaration of inde-pendence from secular and ghostly power, Stephen reaches his sublime. He is then promptly knocked down by Joyce's irony and by Private Carr.

In staging his book's climax in the brothel, the house of climaxes, Joyce took great interest in the flower, Moly, which enables Odysseus to thwart the wiles of Circe and keep her from turning him into a pig. The most literal expression of Moly is Bloom's potato, his grandmother's talisman against disease to which the usually unsuperstitious Bloom clings; it is taken from him by Zoe and his demand to have it back is one sign of his recovery from Bella's spellbinding. Joyce consulted many friends about Moly, and finally wrote Budgen his decision, which proved more inclusive than exclusive: 'Moly is the gift of Hermes, god of public ways, and is the invisible influence (prayer, chance, agility, *presence of mind*, power of recuperation) which saves in case of accident. This would cover immunity from syphilis (συ φιλις = swine-love?). . . . In this special case his plant may be said to have many leaves, indifference due to masturbation, pessimism congenital, a sense of the ridiculous, sudden fastidiousness in some detail, experience.' These qualities are present, but they stick close to the literal sense of the narrative and are not all-inclusive. In Stephen the saving grace is none of them but 'the intellectual imagination', which preserves him from surrender to mother Dedalus, mother church, mother Ireland, mother England, all demanding his filial allegiance. It does not, however, keep him from undergoing, like Bloom at the end of the Cyclops, physical abuse. And when Stephen is unconscious, Joyce invokes a virtue of the emotions rather than of the intellect, somewhat as Tolstoy's Pierre absorbs from Karatayev the heart's reasons.

Bloom is the bearer of this ethic. Joyce draws upon Christ's parable of the Good Samaritan to make Bloom's unassuming act of comradeliness an instance of *Agape*. Bloom secures the help of Corny Kelleher, the undertaker, whose symbolical presence probably implies the burial of the old Stephen. Beaten up and friendless, Stephen is helped by a stranger, whose *acte gratuit* redeems the universe from the chilliness of isolated particles and stamps it as irrevocably gregarious. It is timeless and parabolic. The word known to all men which Stephen had vainly asked his mother is now revealed, though not named. It is love.

Bending down by Stephen, Bloom for the first and only time in the book calls him by his first name. Dante is only once called by name in *The Divine Comedy*, and that is when Beatrice consoles him for the departure of Virgil. In this equally crucial moment, Bloom listens to Stephen's murmuring,

> Who . . . drive . . . Fergus now,
> And pierce . . . wood's woven shade? . . .

and mishears: 'Face reminds me of his poor mother. In the shady wood. The deep white breast. Ferguson, I think I caught. A girl. Some girl. Best thing could happen him . . .' This quotation, coming at the climax of *Ulysses*, recalls the earlier quotation of the same poem in the first episode. There Stephen remembers having sung Yeats's song about Fergus to his dying mother, 'She was crying in her wretched bed. For those words, Stephen: love's bitter mystery.' In retrospect, Joyce seems to have intended those words as the solemn first mention of what was to emerge as his book's ultimate meaning. He had an analogue in the way that Virgil, appearing to Dante at the beginning of *The Divine Comedy*, declared that he had been sent to him by Beatrice, who was moved to do so by love. The role of love becomes steadily more important in Dante as in Joyce. But in comparison with Dante's many cantos devoted to the subject, Joyce is circumspect and scarcely uses the word at all.

That a poem by Yeats should be quoted in this all-important context is probably not without further implication. At the end of *A Portrait*, too, Stephen in his crucial diary recalled a poem of Yeats originally entitled, 'Michael

Robartes Remembers Forgotten Beauty', and said, 'Michael Robartes desires to press in his arms the beauty that has long faded from the world. Not this. Not at all. I desire to press in my arms the beauty that has not yet come into the world.' There, as here in *Ulysses*, Yeats appears as a forerunner, a Virgil to Joyce's Dante, who can accompany Stephen through Purgatory, but cannot go beyond it. (Yeats, like Virgil in *The Divine Comedy*, is not involved in the last section.) Joyce was much concerned with the idea of a precursor: in his youthful letter to Ibsen he assigned that role to Ibsen, then, in 'The Day of the Rabblement', to Ibsen and Hauptmann; but his final decision was for Yeats.

Dante probably lurks behind Bloom's comic mishearing of Fergus as Miss Ferguson, 'a girl', which gives her the role of an imaginary Beatrice, shadowy counterpart of the one who appears in the last cantos of the *Purgatorio*. The intertwining of Yeats's love song with Stephen's memories of his mother acts as a palliative for his previous rejection of her tyrannous ghost. The various forms of love begin to combine into a crowned knot.

The seal upon Bloom's Good Samaritan act is given at the end of the episode by his vision of Rudy, dwarflike Rudy who died at eleven days but is now made whole, 'a fairy boy of eleven'. Each triad ends with a recovery of life, and this one above all. Bloom raises Rudy from the dead like Lazarus, brings him across Lethe in the way that Stephen bragged that ghosts, summoned by his art, would troop over Lethe. Like Christ, or Orpheus, or Odysseus, Bloom harrows hell. The child reading Hebrew from right to left creates by his bizarre attitude and detachment a sense of distance and estrangement from Bloom even as he answers his call. (In Dante's *Purgatorio* Matilda also keeps a distance, on the other side of the river.) Rudy's ivory cane transfigures Stephen's ashplant. He is like a statuette of a child, something to buy it may be in Woolworth's, and yet the effect is not maudlin, but genuinely tender. At the midpoint of the *Wandering Rocks* Lenehan had said that there was 'a touch of the artist about old Bloom', and it is as an artist that he now vindicates himself, creating out of love an image which has independent life. Earlier in the day he remembered his lovemaking with Molly, and recreated it in his imagination. Here, out of love for his dead child, he does more than remember, he reshapes Rudy's misshapen features and raises him from the grave. He fathers and mothers this new-old child. This is not the art of Michelangelo, it may be closer to Grandma Moses, but it is art nonetheless. Bloom's rescue of Stephen was motivated by *Agape*, which is the requisite of art as of nature, his vision of Rudy, sired by paternal love but borne maternally out of memory and desire, is Bloom's way of damning death (as Stephen damned it) and of making life easter in us. Against the corruptions of life and death which had been specified by Stephen in the first part of the book, this second part concludes with resurrection. Freed from supernatural trappings, Bloom and Stephen offer profane salvation, The New Bloomusalem.

In their respective ways they have killed priest and king, have conquered tyranny by imaginative love. Christ sanctified himself; Dante, said Virgil late in the *Purgatorio*, might now be crowned and mitred over himself; Prometheus threw off his bonds. For all three the liberating agent is ultimately love, that Moly of body and soul together, and in its spiritual aspect this is exemplified by Bloom's two acts of resurrection. Stephen and Bloom have approached the state which Joyce announced to Linati was 'fusion', and like Dante are now ready to come out to the stars.

VIII

The New Bloomusalem

Bloom must return home, and *Ulysses* disclose its final meaning. The 'fusion' that Joyce spoke of now occurs between Stephen and Bloom – not atomic but Adamic fusion: together they must form between them the new Adam and convey intimations of a terrestrial paradise. But to do so another element is needed, and this is Molly, who constitutes the third in a new, three-in-one being, a human improvement upon the holy family as upon the divine trinity. To confirm it, she is accorded the same birthday as the Virgin Mary.

So solemn a convergence awakened all Joyce's capacity for comedy. He changed pitch abruptly from the *Circe* episode, where he had displayed the mastery of two kingdoms, of death and birth, when Bloom rescues Stephen from authority in this world and rescues Rudy from the authority of the next. After this fanfaronade which made earth's foundations tremble, the world without end wobbles back, much the worse for wear. With it come space and time, though Stephen announced in *Circe* their annihilation. If Hume's scepticism made possible their upheaval, Joyce perhaps implies – in this spirited canter into philosophy – that they return under the aegis of Kant as conditions of perception rather than properties of things. They are taken back only under sufferance, however, and in the end are forced to retire once more.

A Fiction Not Supreme (16)

The first of the final triad of episodes, *Eumaeus*, still reels from the great events in *Circe*. It is written in a style which Joyce called relaxed; it is also a constabular style – Dogberry's, as it struggles clumsily for the right expression and invariably hits one that is inept as well as stereotyped. Bloom's bloomisms, which were only occasional heretofore, now become continuous. He appears much reduced from that heroic rescuer and artist we saw at the end of the brothel scene. Not being able to keep up with Stephen intellectually, yet eager to do so, he puts himself at a disadvantage. Part of the trouble is fatigue: he is fagged out, and so is the language which describes him. Fatigue makes him seem old, and old age dominates throughout these last chapters, as youth dominated in the first three chapters of the book. Molly is old too, in comparison with Stephen (as well as with Gerty MacDowell, the only other female monologuist), though she is to be rejuvenated. Stephen himself sings at the end of *Eumaeus* Sweelinck's song, 'Youth here has End', as if 16 June divided his youth from his age. (The same song is used for the same purpose in *Giacomo Joyce*.) The next chapters participate in this geriatric spectacle: Joyce described *Ithaca* as done in a 'pacified style', and the formal catechism there is a creaky, senile development of the question-and-answering in Mr Deasy's school. *Penelope*, he said, was done in a 'resigned style'. He emphasized this quality by his description of *Eumaeus* to Linati as in a 'relaxed prose' and to Gilbert as 'Narrative (old)'.

In these episodes Joyce subjects fusion to anatomizing. A guardedness about emotional commitment was a lifelong characteristic and he did not allow his book to contain so climactic a relation without ample demurrer. Bloom's unassuming decency begins and ends *Eumaeus*, but is withered a little by the style: 'Preparatory to anything else Mr Bloom brushed off the greater bulk of the shavings and handed Stephen the hat and ashplant and bucked him up generally in orthodox Samaritan fashion, which he very badly needed.' Since the Samaritans were conspicuously *outside* orthodoxy, that being important to Christ's meaning, 'orthodox Samaritan fashion' is not only a cliché, but an absurdity. The use of the word 'Samaritan' nonetheless points up the parabolic quality of Bloom's act.

In *Eumaeus* wrongheadedness, a principle Joyce largely extracted from Homer, animates the narrative. When Odysseus, still asleep, was laid on the Ithacan shore by the Phaeacian sailors, he woke and did not at first know where he was. Athena appeared to give him his bearings and advice on how to proceed. He donned beggar's rags as a disguise, and then went to meet his loyal swineherd Eumaeus. Biding his time, he offered a cock-and-bull story to explain who he was and how he came to be in Ithaca. Eumaeus doubted the story but offered hospitality anyway, his openness being contrasted with his master's disingenuousness. Joyce developed this contrast of candour and duplicity, of Ulysses enforcing his identity by denying it.

Duplicity leads to the presentation of experience in an assortment of doubles. At the beginning and end of the episode, Bloom cautions Stephen about Mulligan's double-dealing. Only one of Stephen's 'pubhunting *confrères*', Lynch, has stayed with him, says Bloom; 'And that one was Judas', says Stephen. The two men take a wrong turning and therefore must *double back* through labyrinthine Dublin. Even their

conversation retraces the same words. ('You suspect that I may
be important because I belong to ... Ireland ... But I suspect
that Ireland must be important because it belongs to me', is an
example.) Things are not what they seem, nor people either.
They meet Lord John Corley, who is not really a lord; he
asks for a job which he doesn't want; he mistakes Bloom for a
friend of Boylan; offered some pennies, he remarks that they
are really halfcrowns, and when Stephen gives him one, he
promises to pay him back 'some time', by which he means
never. As Bloom and Stephen reach the cabman's shelter,
and hear some Italians talking, Bloom comments on the
'beautiful language'. '*Bella Poetria!*' But *Poetria* is not poetry,
nor Italian, and as for the beauty of the language, Stephen
announces that they were haggling over money.

Inside the cabman's shelter, the doubleness continues. Its
keeper is reputed to be Fitzharris, or Skin-the-Goat, the
man who drove the cab in which the Invincibles escaped after
committing their political murders in the Phoenix Park in
1882. But he is not. He tells the company that Parnell is not
dead and will return, but Parnell lies in Glasnevin. One of
the hangers-on in the shelter looks deceptively like the town
clerk. Bloom and Stephen discuss various examples of
duplicity, false allegation, and error, such as 'Bacon and
Hamlet', ritual murder by Jews (the Protocols of the Elders
of Zion), cases of forged identity (the Tichborne claimant).
Nor are they exempt from any possibility of error themselves,
for Bloom mistakes his man when he addresses Stephen as 'a
good catholic', and in recounting his adventure with the
Citizen in Barney Kiernan's pub, is not above making certain
improvements. The *Evening Telegraph* contributes its share by
journalistic botching of Dignam's funeral. The cabman's
horse, for his part, deposits a trinity of turds on the street

in symbolic counterblow to the three-personed fusion in progress. (He also echoes Mulligan's trinity of eggs in *Telemachus*.) Bloom and Stephen have to avoid these as they go off, even if uneasily, arm in arm. They are described as doing so by some allusions to the song, 'The Low-Backed Car', where the lovers are 'to be married by Father Maher', words which by their inappropriateness continue to mock the fusion of Bloom and Stephen.

Yet they do fuse, in a manner of speaking: 'Though they didn't see eye to eye in everything,' Bloom reflects, 'a certain analogy there somehow was, as if both their minds were travelling, so to speak, in the one train of thought.' They talk about the Sirens' duplicity and about usurpation, two subjects which unite their plights. Running counter to all the doubleness is their tentative singleness. That they are in many ways different does not prevent fusion, any more than the difference in character between Odysseus and his swineherd prevented them from standing together against the suitors' tyranny. They offer a counterpart, in *Agape* or comradeliness, to the evocation in the *Nausicaa* episode of Eros.

The meaning of the episode lies only partly in the union of the two men. Joyce told Linati that the episode's signification was 'The Ambush at Home', a reference to the ambush of Telemachus by the suitors. Joyce extends the reference. The ambusher is the old sailor who in the cabman's shelter occupies the centre of attention. On the narrative level he serves no evident function, but Joyce said that he was Ulysses Pseudangelos, that is, Ulysses the false messenger. In short, he is the false Ulysses, a double. The postcard he carries locates him in Santiago, Chile, and so, like Dante's Ulysses, from whom Joyce here silently dissociates Bloom, he has crossed the Equator. He claims to be a seaman, but Bloom thinks it more likely that he is a convict fresh from prison. The man says his name is W. B. Murphy, which in a land of murphies is like saying it is 'Noman'. He pretends to have a faithful wife who has been waiting for him for seven years, but this Penelope's existence is doubtful. He claims to know Stephen's father, and to have seen him shooting two eggs in a Swedish circus ten years before, and so edges ambiguously into the paternity theme. 'Murphy' has an argosy of stories about his experiences, all of them what Bloom calls 'genuine forgeries'. His significance begins to become clear. What Murphy purveys is a fiction within a fiction, based on an unspoken aesthetic theory, rival to Stephen's, that the novel is a Munchausen performance. With falsisimilitude Murphy would ambush the verisimilitude that is claimed in *Ulysses*, and turn Aristotle's imitation of nature into mere fakery. The sailor is spokesman for false art, for art as *gamesmanship*. If he could, he would deny the significance of this sixteenth episode, and of this sixteenth day of June, as well as the fellowship of Bloom and Stephen, by exhibiting on his chest the tattooed number 16 in token of homosexuality. (This numerical symbolism was, as Gilbert points out, well known on the Continent.) In *Circe* the impulse to love is perverted into the impulse to overcome or be overcome; in *Eumaeus* the sailor would change the impulse of art to create into the pseudo-artistic impulse to gull. The rejection of Murphy attests that *Ulysses* is not a confidence trick. Instead the episode is made to register humbly, among the lying sights and sounds, its sincerity.

La Scienza Nuova e Vecchia (17)

In *Ithaca*, where Bloom is home at last, the pendulum swings in the opposite direction. Instead of subjective distortion there is objective distortion. *Trompe l'œil* gives way to the computer, unreliability to excessive reliability. Reason itself here goes mad, in the ultimate form of the strain of madness which has pervaded the second chapters of each triad. The comedy lies in the patent inadequacy of information-retrieval systems to render the human. It is as if the skeleton had been unfleshed, preparatory to Molly Bloom's fleshing it again. The rocky coast of Ithaca seems also to have given Joyce a scenic hint. He explained to Budgen,

> I am writing *Ithaca* in the form of a mathematical catechism. All events are resolved into their cosmic physical, psychical etc. equivalents, e.g., Bloom jumping down the area, drawing water from the tap, the micturition in the garden, the cone of incense, lighted candle and statue, so that not only will the reader know everything and know it in the baldest coldest way, but Bloom and Stephen thereby become heavenly bodies, wanderers like the stars at which they gaze.

In literal terms, the two characters observe an astronomical event, a shooting star falling from Vega in the Lyre beyond the Tress of Berenice towards the constellation of Leo. The sky, so thunderous in the *Oxen of the Sun*, now offers its distant configuration of a fusion taking place on earth.

Joyce also described this episode as 'the ugly duckling of the book', which means, as William Empson remarks, that it must really be the swan. Opposite to the disorder of *Eumaeus* is the pedantic order here, the arduous particularization of data, the tracing of tapwater to its reservoir source. The mundaneness of the details reflects the habiliments of Ulysses as he first appears in Ithaca, and the pitilessness with which they are laid out evokes the mood of the slaughter of the suitors. By reduction to colourless fact, the imagination is impoverished.

Yet the impoverishment, pursued to its end, begins to dovetail with a 'wealth' of particulars, at least one of which is unexpectedly splendid. With this the episode divides into two parts, of which the first is primarily a divestment of heroic attributes, the second a resumption of them. Stephen and Bloom go out into the garden to urinate, and Joyce takes the occasion of this expression of physical corruption to have them see in the fertile sky 'The heaventree of stars hung with humid nightblue fruit.' Here the phrasing is totally unscientific: Bloom anatomizes this description of the sky a few pages later and laboriously concludes that it is not really a heaventree. But the comparison has been made, the tree of life in an earthly paradise has found its emblem, and nature is more than the statistics about it. The sky translates into fluent heavenspeech the awkward, broken accents of earth.

The episode has in fact a number of affirmations to make, including the affirmation of affirmation. At the start Stephen and Bloom disagree about literature and civic self-help; the latter is a particular interest of Bloom's but not of Stephen's. For the first, Stephen asserts that literature is the eternal affirmation of the spirit of man, the most eloquent thing he has been willing to say about it. (Bloom tacitly disagrees, presumably because for him literature is chiefly a more local attempt to 'move or touch' by emotional poignancy.) From this Stephen counters Bloom's dark thoughts about the imperfectibility of life by affirming 'his significance as a conscious rational animal proceeding syllogistically from the

known to the unknown and a conscious rational reagent between a micro- and a macrocosm ineluctably constructed
upon the incertitude of the void'. Such a blend of Aristotle
and Hume is suited to this painfully rational chapter, though
it is not an adequate definition for man as expounded in the
book as a whole. Bloom's final affirmation is achieved with
great difficulty, as he slaughters his scruples about cuckoldry.
For this conquest his great bow shoots two arrows. One is at
purity. Here his conclusion is that life consists of a series of
sexual excitations, so that no one can ever reasonably suppose
that another person's sexual life begins and ends with him.
The second arrow is shot at his jealousy of Boylan, and here
too the method is to enlarge the context until the particular
act of 'matrimonial outrage' is put in cosmic perspective. In
this way Bloom masters soul and body. His conclusion is that
fidelity and infidelity coincide, being admixed in every relationship. As D. H. Lawrence says, we are 'free/To be faithful
and faithless together/As we have to be'. Having solved his
rational problems, Bloom makes himself comfortable beside
his wife's bodily warmth.

He and Molly lie in bed, in opposite directions. She is
positioned as Gea-Tellus, but she is also everywoman. Bloom
lies in a foetal position, 'the childman weary, the manchild
in the womb', fusing embryo and adult. As he falls off, 'Going
to a dark bed there was a square round Sinbad the Sailor roc's
auk's egg in the night of the bed of all the auks of the rocs of
Darkinbad the Brightdayler.' It would seem that Bloom has
squared the circle, which indicates that he is not sleeping
only 'Newton's sleep', in spite of the Newtonian geometry
of circles, squares, parallel lines, and the like that pervade
the chapter. The final question is 'Where?' and the answer is
a point. A point is that which has no parts, and Bloom's

THE

LEOPOLD SHAKSPERE.

The Poet's Works, in Chronological Order,

FROM THE TEXT OF PROFESSOR DELIUS,

WITH

"THE TWO NOBLE KINSMEN" AND "EDWARD III.,"

AND

AN INTRODUCTION BY F. J. FURNIVALL.

Illustrated.

CASSELL PETTER & GALPIN:

LONDON, PARIS & NEW YORK.

1877.

Title-page of the *Leopold Shakspere*, an edition by F. J. Furnivall, 1877.

Rembrandt, *Aristotle Contemplating the Bust of Homer*, 1653.

Hans Baldung Grien, *Aristotle and Phyllis*, 1513. (Reproduced from A. Bartsch, *Le Peintre-Graveur*, VII, p. 317, no. 48.)

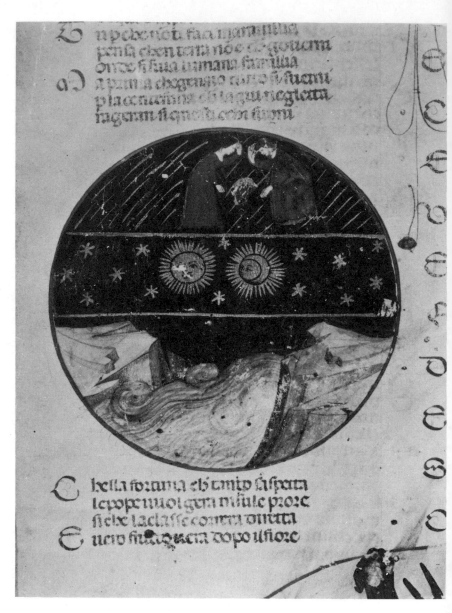

Dante and Beatrice looking down on the Straits of Gibraltar (*Paradiso*, Canto XXVII).
From a late-fourteenth-century illuminated manuscript in the Biblioteca Marciana,
Venice.

completeness is implied. But earlier a star was described as no more than a pinprick, and this is a pinprick too, which may be taken as the earth itself as seen from interstellar space. For while the sky had been restored in the heaventree of stars, the earth is yet to be rotated in Molly's final chapter, where its motion symbolizes Penelope's weaving. Finally, the earth may be considered the point of the book, as well as of the *Ithaca* chapter.

Why Molly Bloom Menstruates (18)

The denouement of Ulysses has been much disputed. What seems to end the book is that Bloom, who nodded off at the end of the *Ithaca* episode, and his more wakeful wife Molly, both snore away in the arms of Morpheus, or as Joyce puts it, in the arms of Murphy. But is this really the end? Did Joyce have no future in mind for his characters? The question is particularly likely to be asked because *A Portrait* is often said to find its sequel in *Ulysses* where Stephen appears after an interval of about two years. But *A Portrait* seems self-contained, it celebrates the birth first of Stephen's body and then of his soul, it brings him from inchoate to real selfhood, from possibility to decision. If he reappears in *Ulysses*, and I won't deny that he does, he is there for a different purpose, not to present his further adventures.

What then does happen to Bloom and Stephen? One critic declares that Stephen goes out into the night and writes — *Ulysses*. But *Ulysses* is not the work of Stephen, any more than *Hamlet* is the work of Hamlet; it issues from that mind of which Stephen, Bloom, Molly, and even Mulligan and Boylan are only aspects. Two other critics regard the ending as proleptic, but the events they foresee are not the same. William Empson remembers that Stephen, after refusing to stay the night, agrees to exchange with Mrs Bloom Italian for singing lessons, and proposes that Stephen returns on 17 June or anyway in the next few days, with his grammar book. The mutual instruction then takes a predictable turn. Bloom tolerates the affair, Empson feels, because he wants desperately to have a son, even if through the agency of another man.

On a practical level, this theory offers a number of difficulties. Apart from Molly's impending concert tour, which will make other alliances than with Boylan complicated for her, Empson leans heavily upon what appears to be a mere gesture of politeness on Stephen's part. Having been rescued from a jam, and having turned down an invitation to stay the night, he avoids twice refusing his host pointblank by appearing to accept a vague and unscheduled exchange of lessons. But Bloom recognizes – and Joyce at once underlines the recognition – that Stephen's return is problematic. That Molly dandles the idea as an erotic fancy does not make it more likely. The notion of a Stephen–Molly affair outside the book is so skimpily supported that it becomes a nineteenth-century parlour game like, 'Describe Desdemona's girlhood' or 'Fortinbras's reign in Denmark'.

The other theory for 17 June is exactly opposite. According to it, Bloom, instead of relaxing further his marriage tie, tightens it and becomes a proper husband. Edmund Wilson proposed this idea some years ago in an uncharacteristic burst of optimism; he contended that Bloom's request for breakfast in bed proved that Bloom was once more becoming master in his own house. A difficulty with this oatmeal theory is that it rests heavily upon the notion that not to make breakfast himself is Bloom's assertion of male authority. This in turn would be more convincing if Bloom had seemed put upon when he made breakfast on the morning of June 16, but actually he likes cooking and doesn't feel degraded by it. Moreover he has apparently done it, except when ill, during the whole of their married life, including the period when they enjoyed complete conjugal relations. Need he feel degraded? After all, if cooks are always women, chefs are always men. His request for breakfast may be just what it appears to be, an expression of fatigue after a late night which is most unusual for him. Molly indicates that she expects to return to the usual pattern after one morning's exertions. At any rate, it seems an unwarranted assumption that breakfast in bed will restore anyone's sexual relations to normalcy. It is harder to reject Wilson's theory than Empson's but both suffer from a desire, vestigial even among modern readers of novels, to detain the characters a little longer in their fictional lives. Yet a warning must be taken from Eugammon of Cyrene, who tacked his unfortunate sequel on to the *Odyssey*.

Joyce declared in his aesthetic notebook that the excellence of a comedy depended upon its joy, which in turn depended upon its fulfilment of desire. To the extent that a work was not sufficient to itself, it was deficient in joy. He could scarcely then have intended to encourage speculation about the future of his characters. He meant what he said in a letter, that in the *Ithaca* episode Bloom and Stephen become like the stars at which they gaze, and that in *Penelope* Bloom and Molly with him are off to eternity. The conjugal future at 7 Eccles street no longer interests him, any more than future doings of Odysseus and Penelope interest Homer or of Dante and Beatrice interest the author of *The Divine Comedy*. Joyce leaves possibilities at the end like dangling threads, just as Homer leaves an unfulfilled prophecy of Tiresias, but he has his mind set on other things. At the end of his Linati schema Joyce shows Bloom going off to '*Alta Notte*' ('Deep Night') and Stephen to '*Alba*' ('Dawn'), but since these opposites coincide the point is that there is no more to say. If Joyce had wanted to, he could certainly have given the book either Empson's or Wilson's conclusion: to please Empson he might have let Stephen stay the night, to please Wilson he could have had husband and wife resume complete sexual relations for the first time in eleven years. He does neither of these, though in Homer Telemachus presumably sleeps in the palace and Odysseus and Penelope share a bed. Instead of sexual intercourse in the present, Joyce has Molly think of a sexual scene in the past. He did so not because Flaubert had prescribed to the writer of fiction, *ne pas conclure*, but because he had another conclusion in mind.

He said himself that 'The last word (human, all too human) is left to Penelope. This is the indispensable countersign to Bloom's passport to eternity.' Beyond eternity his characters could scarcely be expected to go. The episode was, he said, the book's *clou*, the nail that drove it into place. In a jocular mood he said also that *Ithaca* was the true ending of the book because *Penelope* had neither beginning, middle, nor end. But it is not so formless as that, since it begins with a capital letter and ends with a fullstop. Moreover, the first word in the book is *Stately* and the last *Yes*, the first and last letters of each being reversed so that the serpent has his tail in his mouth at last. It would be more accurate to say that the form of *Penelope* is ungirdled than that it is nonexistent. Molly's countersign may be deciphered, and an explanation given for her thoughts of Mrs Riordan, an elderly widow now dead, for her menstruation, and for her memories of adolescence on Gibraltar. These prove necessary rather than improvisatory.

Coming after the dry, impersonal, and pseudo-scientific order of most of the *Ithaca* episode, the final monologue offers a personal, lyrical efflorescence. It is the only episode to which Joyce assigns no specific hour – the time is no o'clock, or as he said in one schema, it is the time indicated mathematically by the slightly disproportioned figure ∞ or lemniscate lying on its side – the number of eternity and infinity. It might be more exact to say that the ruins of time and space and the mansions of eternity here coexist, at least until the very end. Molly presents herself without portentousness as spokesman for nature. Like the Wife of Bath, she contends that God has not endowed us with sensual proclivities if these are not to be indulged. 'Nature it is', she insists, falling into the fallacy of identifying virtue with what is natural that Hume had criticized. (Joyce too knew it was a fallacy; Richard Rowan in *Exiles*, when Robert poses a 'law of nature', retorts, 'Did I vote it?') Yet Molly's nature is not indiscriminate; as she sees and represents it, nature is choosy – Darwin thought it choosy too. Still she is acceptant enough to plant the almost desert globe of the *Ithaca* episode with vegetables and people and animals and curious objects. Most of all, she covers it with flowers. In the Linati plan the part of the body allotted to *Penelope* is fat (*Eumaeus* having offered nerves, and *Ithaca* bones). Philosophy is fleshed. Stephen had recalled earlier the medieval legend that Aristotle was enticed by a 'light o' love' to let her bit, bridle, and ride him, and Molly's nature, so much more earthy, trivial, sexualized, and lyrical than Aristotle's or Hume's, appears as a final penetration by the wisdom of the body of the wisdom of the mind. (Molly's only acquaintance with Aristotle is the apocryphal and semi-pornographic *Aristotle's Masterpiece*; she malaprops his name into 'some old Aristocrat or whatever his name is'.) '*Ich bin das Fleisch das stets bejaht*', Joyce says of her, confirming her as the opposite pole to Mulligan's denying spirit. But her yeasaying is mixed with much naysaying – until the very end of her monologue 'Yes' and 'No' (with a great many 'knows' for good measure) are rivals for pre-eminence. Her final affirmation is a victory over strong resistance.

Molly Bloom's birthday is 8 September, and in tribute to this anniversary, and to the symbol of eternity-infinity, Joyce writes her monologue in eight sentences. 'It begins and ends', Joyce wrote Budgen,

> with the female word *yes*. It turns like the huge earth ball slowly surely and evenly round and round spinning, its four cardinal points being the female breasts, arse, womb and cunt expressed by the words *because*, *bottom* (in all senses bottom button, bottom of the class, bottom of the sea, bottom of his heart), *woman*, *yes*. Though probably more obscene than any preceding episode it seems to me to be perfectly sane full amoral fertilisable untrustworthy engaging shrewd limited prudent indifferent *Weib*.

He delights in mythologizing Molly as Gea-Tellus, then, by bringing her down with a thump onto the orangekeyed chamberpot at 7 Eccles street, in demythologizing her into an old shoe.

Molly's animadversions begin with thoughts of Mrs Riordan, a widow whom Bloom befriended:

> Yes because he never did a thing like that before as ask to get his breakfast in bed with a couple of eggs since the *City Arms* hotel when he used to be pretending to be laid up with a sick voice doing his highness to make himself interesting to that

old faggot Mrs Riordan that he thought he had a great leg of
and she never left us a farthing all for masses for herself and
her soul greatest miser ever was actually afraid to lay out 4d
for her methylated spirit telling me all her ailments she had
too much old chat in her about politics and earthquakes and
the end of the world let us have a bit of fun first God help the
world if all the women were her sort down on bathingsuits
and lownecks of course nobody wanted her to wear I suppose
she was pious because no man would look at her twice I
hope Ill never be like her a wonder she didnt want us to
cover our faces . . . [723; 871]

Joyce's purpose is served by having Molly establish her own
point of view against its counterpart, Mrs Riordan's prudery,
the latter associated with miserliness and piety here, as
earlier in the book with occultism and aestheticism. Molly
might seem to run more danger from the opposite faction, of
Mistress Moll Flanders. She says herself, however, that she is
not a whore or a slut, and she is right. Only the most rigor-
ous interpretation of adultery – Christ's in the Sermon on
the Mount, 'Whosoever looketh on a woman to lust after her
hath committed adultery with her already in his heart' –
could consider Molly's friendships, except that with Boylan,
and perhaps that with D'Arcy, as adulterous. The book
makes clear that this first relationship is something new.
June 16 may in fact be the first day that Boylan and Molly
have had 'carnal', as Bloom puts it. It may also be, though this
is never established, the day in June that Bloom and Molly
climaxed their courtship by proposal and consent among the
rhododendrons on Howth sixteen years before. Joyce plays
on the coincidence without bearing down too hard. Fidelity
and infidelity coexist.

Essentially Molly is right about herself – she is not the

wholly sexual being that to Boylan she must appear to be. She hopes that he is pleased with her, but she is not really pleased with him. She complains about his too familiar manners in slapping her on the behind – 'I'm not a horse or an ass am I' – but she remembers that Boylan's father was a horsetrader and hopes this fact may explain his conduct. Boylan writes bad loveletters ending, 'Yours ever Hugh Boylan'. Molly detects that he is basically a 'strange brute' with an unconscionableness that Stephen had earlier described as the *sentimental* desire to 'enjoy without incurring the immense debtorship for a thing done'. So while Molly is not planning to break with Boylan, she is not expecting the relationship to last, and thinks of other men as more perceptive and congenial. For the same reason she rejects sado-masochism, in books about flagellants, 'Sure theres nothing for a woman in that.' She steers between Mrs Riordan's masochistic prudery and Boylan's loutishness.

Bloom has as much trouble as Ulysses had in winning recognition as Penelope's husband. Joyce complained once of his wife that she did not appear to see much difference between him and other men, though in fact Nora Joyce remarked to a friend that her husband was like nobody else. The seeming (though not real) inability to differentiate finely is characteristic of Molly, who falls into calling the various men she has known by the pronoun 'he', without much further identification. (Stephen Dedalus did the same in *Proteus*: 'She she she. What she?' But he had no particular woman to think about.) Against Stephen's effort to make women mythical, 'handmaidens of the moon', 'wombs of sin', and the like, Molly regards men as either natural or unnatural. Basically she is earth to Bloom's sun, modifying his light by her own movements. She is thoroughly aware of his many failings, but notes also a few virtues. He is kind to old women like Mrs Riordan, he has a few brains, he was handsome when young, he wipes his feet on the mat. On the other hand, his atheism, his socialism, his talk of persecution, put her off. She gradually acknowledges his pre-eminence by the frequency with which she returns to thinking about him. As compared with Boylan, her husband is the more complete man, with the supreme virtue that he wishes her well. She cannot say as much for Boylan. Molly, as the earth, prefers in Bloom the more complete to the less complete example of a biological species.

In the book's characterology, Molly is needed to contribute a quality not often present in either Bloom or Stephen, her naturalness and spontaneity. The two men are thoughtful, detached, Bloom because he sees all round, Stephen because he looks deep in. Molly's monologue is therefore less an addition than a correction. The *Ithaca* episode had offered a heliocentric view of Bloom, Molly offers a geocentric one, the two together forming the angle of parallax (a word which had baffled Bloom earlier in the day). Bloomsday becomes everymansday, and everywomansday, in that all necessary elements of desirable life have been gathered together. None of the principal figures is complete in himself, but together they sum up what is affirmable. At the end we are brought back to the earth, to spring, to vegetation, and to sexual love.

Molly has a capacity for intense yet fastidious feeling which makes Joyce's altitudinous ending possible. The peroration of her monologue is morose delectation, theologically speaking, but moroseness plays no part in it. She is thinking of that day among the rhododendrons on Howth when she and Bloom came to an understanding, but she marvellously collocates such elements as land and sea to have them all 'swimming in roses'.

> I love flowers Id love to have the whole place swimming in roses God of heaven theres nothing like nature the wild mountains then the sea and the waves rushing then the beautiful country with fields of oats and wheat and all kinds of things and all the fine cattle going about that would do your heart good to see rivers and lakes and flowers all sorts of shapes and smells and colours springing up even out of the ditches primroses and violets nature it is

She quickly resolves the questions of belief and incertitude which have dogged Stephen and western philosophy, and with which Bloom has bothered her, by finding them not worth asking:

> as for them saying theres no God I wouldnt give a snap of my two fingers for all their learning why dont they go and create something I often asked him atheists or whatever they call themselves go and wash the cobbles off themselves first then they go howling for the priest and they dying and why why because theyre afraid of hell on account of their bad conscience ah yes I know them well who was the first person in the universe before there was anybody that made it all who ah that they dont know neither do I so there you are they might as well try to stop the sun from rising tomorrow the sun shines for you he said the day we were lying among the rhododendrons on Howth head in the grey tweed suit and his straw hat the day I got him to propose to me yes first I gave him the bit of seedcake out of my mouth and it was leapyear like now yes 16 years ago

This recollection of the seedcake, which Bloom also experienced in the *Lestrygonians* episode, is vaguely reminiscent of something else, and if we remember that *Finnegans Wake* speaks of the apple in the Garden of Eden as the seedfruit, there is a momentary connection with the apple which Eve passed to Adam as Molly to Bloom. This is what St Augustine called the happy fault, *felix culpa*, but Bloom calls it *copula felix*, happy not because it brought about redemption by Christ, but in itself. As in Dante's Earthly Paradise, Adam and Eve have been absolved of original sin. Moist with spittle, the seedcake offers its parallel also to the host, and the lovers' rite is contrasted with the black mass of *Circe*.

> my God after that long kiss I near lost my breath yes he said I was a flower of the mountain yes so we are flowers all a womans body yes that was one true thing he said in his life and the sun shines for you today yes that was why I liked him because I saw he understood or felt what a woman is and I knew I could always get round him and I gave him all the pleasure I could leading him on till he asked me to say yes and I wouldnt answer first only looked out over the sea and the sky I was thinking of so many things he didnt know of Mulvey and Mr Stanhope and Hester and father and old captain Groves and the sailors playing all birds fly and I say stoop and washing up dishes they called it on the pier and the sentry in front of the governors house with the thing round his white helmet poor devil half roasted and the Spanish girls laughing in their shawls and their tall combs and the auctions in the morning the Greeks and the jews and the Arabs and the devil knows who else from all the ends of Europe and Duke street

Duke street is in Dublin. East and West join here, as in *Circe* greekjew and jewgreek meet, with the Arabs added here to the pot:

> and the fowl market all clucking outside Larby Sharons and the poor donkeys slipping half asleep and the vague fellows

in the cloaks asleep in the shade on the steps and the big wheels of the carts of the bulls and the old castle thousands of years old yes and those handsome Moors all in white and turbans like kings asking you to sit down in their little bit of a shop and Ronda with the old windows of the posadas glancing eyes a lattice hid for her lover to kiss the iron and the wineshops half open at night and the castanets and the night we missed the boat at Algeciras the watchman going about serene with his lamp and O that awful deepdown torrent O and the sea the sea crimson sometimes like fire [766–8; 932]

Water and fire combine, and so does the crimson sea of the straits of Gibraltar with Molly's menstruation, about which she has complained earlier, as if the natural forces of earth and woman were synonymous. This synthesis was prepared long before in the book; in the *Proteus* episode Stephen brooded on the oddity of God's transubstantiation into flesh occurring in so many communions in so many times and places:

And at the same instant perhaps a priest round the corner is elevating it. Dringdring! And two streets off another locking it into a pyx. Dringadring! And in a ladychapel another taking housel all to his own cheek. Dringdring! Down, up, forward, back. [41; 49]

Then in *Nausicaa* Bloom meditated on the same identity-variety in the process of menstruation:

How many women in Dublin have it today? Martha, she [Gerty]. Something in the air. That's the moon. But then why don't all women menstruate at the same time with same moon, I mean? Depends on the time they were born, I suppose. Or all start scratch then get out of step. [361; 479]

These two passages seem at first to be idle. But Joyce is establishing a secret parallel and opposition: the body of God and the body of woman share blood in common. In allowing Molly to menstruate at the end Joyce consecrates the blood in the chamberpot rather than the blood in the chalice, mentioned by Mulligan at the beginning of the book. For this blood is substance, not more or less than substance. The great human potentiality is substantiation, not transubstantiation, or subsubstantiation. It is this quality which the artist has too, in that he produces living human characters, not ethereal or less than human ones. It is human blood, not divine. Menstruation is Promethean.

> and the glorious sunsets and the figtrees in the Alameda gardens yes and all the queer little streets and pink and blue and yellow houses and the rosegardens and the jessamine and geraniums and cactuses and Gibraltar as a girl where I was a Flower of the mountain yes when I put the rose in my hair like the Andalusian girls used or shall I wear a red yes and how he kissed me under the Moorish wall

Molly confuses, or rather conflates, an incident when in her early youth she lay on the rock of Gibraltar beside Lieutenant Mulvey, with the moment of her courtship by Bloom on another eminence, the hill of Howth.

And now her reference to all the men she has known as 'he' has a sudden relevance: Mulvey glides into Bloom in the next line: 'and I thought well as well him as another'. In Homer Tiresias had prophesied that Ulysses would, after some years with Penelope, set sail once again but return at last to Ithaca. Dante, however, as Keats said, brought 'news' of Ulysses, for in the *Inferno* Ulysses tells Dante of a last, presumptuous voyage beyond the pillars of Hercules and out

into the unknown and for him fatal sea. In Molly's mind
Mulvey, who was her Ulysses on Calpe's mount at Gibraltar,
blends into Bloom, her Ulysses on Howth. She stamps an
Irish visa on Ulysses' Greek passport. There is also an Italian
visa, for Dante and Beatrice in Canto XXVII of the *Paradiso*
look down on the straits of Gibraltar just as Bloom-Mulvey
and Molly do. It is now clear why Molly Bloom had to be
born so far from Ireland, at the pillars of Hercules.

In the last non-sentences of her monologue Molly, having
as she said got Bloom to propose to her, joins activity to
passivity, aggression to surrender:

> and I thought well as well him as another and then I asked
> him with my eyes to ask again yes and then he asked me would
> I yes to say yes my mountain flower and first I put my arms
> around him yes and drew him down to me so he could feel
> my breasts all perfume yes and his heart was going like mad
> and yes I said yes I will Yes. [768; 933]

But why then does Molly end with an act of sixteen years
before? She seems to burst the confines of her present situation, and fly from her jingly bed to a time which is beyond
present time and a place beyond present place. In fact, she
bursts through them to 'that other world' mentioned by
Martha Clifford, which is not death but an imaginative
recreation, like *le temps retrouvé* of Proust. Like Adam and
Eve's, it is a paradise lost, for as Proust says the only true
paradise is the one we have lost. According to Dante, Adam
and Eve's paradise lasted only six hours, Bloom and Molly's
is about the same. At the beginning of Molly's monologue
she had thought of Mrs Riordan predicting the end of the
world, and here, in memory and imagination, the world
does end and is created afresh. Joyce said that this episode

had no art, but his book is consummated by the principle
that art is nature's self. Molly, like Gerty MacDowell, like
Bloom, like Stephen, has a touch of the artist about her, but
that is because art is a natural process, which begins and ends
with impure substance, and bids the dead to rise. There is
sadness too, since Molly's present is so bleak in comparison
with that lost paradise where, as Yeats said, all was 'blossom-
ing and dancing'. The sadness is muted, however. Time and
space are, at least for an instant, mere ghosts beside eternity
and infinity.

Not Stephen then – though he defined the eucharistic
element of art – but Molly, re-bears paradise, and Bloom,
who earlier evoked the same scene, is her husband in art as in
law. But Joyce has other nuptials in mind as well. *Penelope*
ends the second half of the book as *Scylla and Charybdis* ended
the first. The idea that Stephen brought to birth in *Scylla* is
that Shakespeare's life provided him with the matter of his
plays and poems, or in grander terms, that art is nature.
Molly, by demonstrating that nature is art, may be seen as
reaching across nine chapters of the book to offer Shakespeare her hand. As Shakespeare says in *A Winter's Tale*, 'o'er
that art/Which you say adds to nature is an art/That nature
makes.' Deliberate and spontaneous creation are joined.

As if to render this contract more licit, Joyce in the *Circe*
episode had Bloom and Stephen look together into a mirror,
and see there not their own faces but the beardless face of
Shakespeare. The cuckolded Shakespeare and Bloom, and
Stephen the betrayed, are more closely akin than anyone
would have suspected. All three out of victimization, as
Molly out of present deprivation, create their artistic
moments. There is a famous late-nineteenth-century edition
of Shakespeare edited by F. J. Furnivall, which is known as the

Leopold Shakespere, and Joyce makes this strange amalgam credible, with Stephen, now fused with Bloom, also a part of it. He announces the nuptials of Mrs Marion Bloom and Mr Leopold Shakespeare.

But another ingredient is necessary for art as for nature. Bloom's statement that the very opposite of hatred is truly life is borne out by Molly's last words, for it is love which empowers the imagination to overcome time, just as it is love which, in Wallace Stevens's words, 'tips the tree of life'. The first nine episodes of the book ended with a vision of the act of love as the basic act of art. The last nine episodes end with a vision of love as the basic act of nature. Joyce affirms this union of the two halves of his book by uniting the ship, which appears so heraldically and mysteriously at the end of the *Telemachiad*, with the straits which appear at the end of the *Return*. The ship sails through the straits, even navigation constituting an amorous movement. The ship is the *Rosevean*, and its name is taken up in Molly's epithalamion where she thinks about wearing a white rose or a red. Thus is fulfilled Stephen's prophecy in the *Oxen of the Sun*, 'Desire's wind blasts the thorntree but after it becomes from a bramblebush to be a rose upon the rood of time.' Yeats, Dante, and Joyce all agree, though Joyce corrects Dante (and Plato) by placing sexual love above all other kinds of love. Red-rosed Molly and Bloom, himself a flower, fertilize the terrestrial paradise. Their youth and age, their innocence and experience, blend. In their dark bed at dead of night the summer sunlight shines.

The narrative level of the book has by this time become less important, and Joyce will not pursue his characters literally because he has negotiated their symbolic reconciliation. On the ethical level Bloom and Stephen have succeeded in

taking the city of Dublin by exposing enthusiasm and superstition there, and by disclosing a truer way of goodwill and
freedom. Molly's hardwon approbation confirms their enterprise. On the historical level, the characters have awakened
from the Circean nightmare of history by drawing the past
into the present (a timeless present) and making it an
expression of love instead of hatred, of fondness rather than
remorse. Art has been shown to be a part of nature, and in
all its processes an imitation of natural ones. These processes
have their summit in love, of which the highest form is
sexual love.

Joyce outflanks the individual lives of his characters by
these ultimate implications. But he outflanks them also by
making each episode a part of the body. It seemed at first that
this slow accretion of a human form was gratuitous, but it
must now be seen to be essential. Stephen says that literature
is the eternal affirmation of the spirit of man, but pure spirit
is something never endorsed in this book. For the body of
man must be affirmed with his spirit. So the pervasive
physicality of *Ulysses* goes with its spirituality. The Identity
of the archetypal man whose body the whole book limns is
never given; it can scarcely be Bloom, since the book is
larger than he, it must include Molly and Stephen, a trinity
and a unity. On the analogy of Blake's giant Albion, the
androgynous man who stands within and behind and beyond
might be called Hibernion. One day he will be Finnegan.

In the final stages of his book Joyce, with all his boldness,
shows a certain embarrassment and reticence. He speaks of
love without naming it; he celebrates art as an essential part
of nature, but offers his proofs without ceremony or explanation; his moral criticism of his time is sharp yet couched
entirely in images; without warning he raises his narrative

from a literal to an anagogic plane. He is determined that his book, unlike some of the works of his master Tolstoy, should not be didactic. What claims he has to make for various possibilities in experience he puts forward with the utmost delicacy. That we are all members of the one body, and of the one spirit, remains implicit rather than explicit. This message he will give us only obliquely and in Greek, in Dublin Greek.

IX

Anatomy of Return

The organization of the last six episodes may be illustrated by
the following tables:

Episode	Contraries	Coinciding by	Product	Antidote	Presiding category	Dominant symbol	Vichian parallels
(13) Nausicaa	Imaginary communion/ imaginary copulation	Concurrence	Imaginary reception of body	Image-breaking	Space	Sand	Age: Theocratic (adoration) Language: Sacred (Latin) Wisdom: Oracular (vaginal and priestly)
	Mariolatry/sentimentality Virgin Mary/Virgin Gerty	'Projected mirage'	Creamy-dreaminess	Detumescence			
	Penis/Roman candle Retreat (spiritual)/ approach (physical) Voyage/Return Forward/Backward Ascent/Descent Erection/Demolition Castles in sand/ castles in the air Youth/Age Novelty/Repetition *Omphalos*/Oracle Bat/Cuckoo	Idolatry	Rapture	Masturbation			

	Analogy	Arm-in-arm ambulation	Fiction	Gamesmanship	True art	Trinity	(sailor's yarns)	(religious discussion, Samaritan, Father Maher)
Pseudangelos								Language: Sacred (Latin)
Bloom/W.B. Murphy								Wisdom: Oracular (prophetic)
Art/False art								
Original/simulacrum								
Corley/Lord John Corley								
Hanger or-/town clerk								
Hamlet (Shakespeare)/Bacon								
Fidelity/infidelity								
Holy Writ/forgeries								
Tichborne heir/Tichborne claimant								
Parnell/Parnell redivivus								
History/False history								
Isolation/Duplicity								
Disciple/Judas								
Bloom/Stephen	Analogy	Arm-in-arm ambulation	Fiction	Gamesmanship	True art	Trinity		

Episode	Contraries	Coinciding by	Product	Antidote	Presiding category	Dominant symbol	Vichian parallels
(14) Oxen of the Sun	Ontogeny/Stylogeny	Recapitulation	Baby, prose work		Time	Vagitus	Age: Aristocratic (kings and popes)
	Gestation (natural)/gestation (artistic)	Similitude	Word as flesh–flesh as word				Language: Symbolic (Word and word)
	Desecration of art/desecration of nature	Mockery	Inhumanity	Goodwill			Wisdom: Devious (Bloom and students)
	Invocation/Deprecation						
	Conception/Contraception	Wild talk	Indifference	Concern			
	Time/Eternity	Creation	Work of art				
	Thorntree/Rosebush						
	Fertility/Sterility						
	King/Pope						
	Sexuality/Holiness						
	England/Ireland						
	Pregnant belly/pregnant word						
	Lightning/Thunder						
	Penetration (Bloom)/emergence (Stephen)						
	Sperm/Embryo						
	Begetting/Parturition						
	Fascism/Anarchy	Vagueness	Chaos	Natural order (of birth, of words)			

	serving, urinating, conversing together		
Comparison/Contrast	Statistics	Separation	Imaginative junction
Candle/Ashplant	Philosophy		
Affirmation/Doubt	Unlocked door	Acceptance	
Key/Keylessness	Reason and fondness	Entrance	
Jealousy/Equanimity		Forgiveness	
Bloom/Molly	Propinquity and affection	Kiss	
Stephen, Bloom, Molly/ Shooting star, Leo, Berenice	Observation	Holy Family	
Square/Circle	Dream	Point	
Sun/Darkness	Sleep	Darkinbad the Brightdayler	
Gea-Tellus, Web	Muliebrity	Old shoe	

(lofty sources, starry spectacles, upper-middle aspirations)
Language: Symbolic (geometry)
Wisdom: Devious (Bloom with Stephen and Molly, Stephen's secret destination)

Episode	Contraries	Coinciding by	Product	Antidote	Presiding category	Dominant symbol	Vichian parallels
(15) Circe	Inner world/Outer world	Penitential surrealism and metempsychosis	Knockdown, putdown	Agape	Beyond space and time	Brothel	Age: Democratic (mélange) Language: Demotic (scatological) Wisdom: Sympathetic (Purgatorial) Ricorso (13–15): Rudy (product of imagination, memory, and love)
	Priest/King	Fear and hatred	Subjugation	Art (imagination and love)			
	Pornosophy/pornography						
	Soul/Body	Symbolic act of Agape	Unity of Being				
	Death/Death in Life	Bloom's mind	Rescue of Stephen, resurrection of Rudy				
	Objects/Persons	Anthropomorphism	Chaos	Moly			
	Persons/Animals	Zoomorphism	Abasement	Moly			
	Nymph/Bella	Double cross	Identity	Reality principle			
	Purity/Vileness						
	Bello/Bella						
	Sado/Masochism						
	Bawd/Cuckold						
	Roses/Bones	Womancity					
	Life/Death	Imaginative memory	Resurrection (Rudy)				
	Mass/Black Mass	God-intoxication	Inhumanity	Artistic transubstantiation			
	Ascension/Abasement						
	British soldiers/Irish	Desire to sub-	Violence	Brotherhood			

Arraignment/coronation						
Criminal/alderman						
Corrupter/reformer						
Bloom/Stephen	Victimization	Fusion				
jewgreek/greekjew			None needed			
Bloom/Stephen	Mirror image, Resilience, imaginative recovery, sympathy	Shakespeare Art				
Blephen/Shakespeare						

(18) Penelope						
Molly/Poldy	Affection	Mutual forgiveness	None needed	Infinity–Eternity	Body astraddle soul	Age: Democratic (everywoman)
Infidelity/Fidelity						Language: Vernacular (natural speech)
Ship/Straits	Navigation	Penetration Interfusion				Wisdom: Sympathetic (acceptance)
East/West	Melting pot					Ricorso (16–18): Sexual love
Gibraltar/Howth	Molly's mind	Ulysses' Irish voyage				
Mulvey/Bloom	Molly's mind	Holy Family, surrogate trinity				
Stephen/Bloom						
Sun/Earth	Imagination	Union of woman and nature				
Day/Night	Colour					
Sea/Menstrual blood		Substance				
Transubstantiation/Menstruation	Human form divine	Infinity–Eternity				
Space/Time	Break through	Spaceless–Timelessness, awakening from nightmare of history				
Imagination/Memory	Love	Ulysses				
Art/Nature	Passion	None desired				

It is possible now to perceive the way in which the whole of *Ulysses* is entwined. In all six triads, the first chapters offer large gestures and reductions of them. *Telemachus* begins with Godsbody and ends with dogsbody, *Calypso* begins with eating and ends with defecating; *Aeolus* proceeds from inflation to deflation, the *Wandering Rocks* from motion to standing still; *Nausicaa* from tumescence to detumescence, and *Eumaeus* from deception to undeception.

The second chapters present instances of cruelty and good-will: in *Nestor*, persecution and anti-persecution; in the *Lotus-Eaters*, masochistic punishment and release from it; in *Lestrygonians*, the killer instinct versus love; in *Sirens*, loss and betrayal in love and war as against more positive emotions; in *Oxen of the Sun*, desecration and celebration; in *Ithaca*, anatomizing and affirming.

The third chapters accomplish their syntheses: *Proteus*, of space and time, human and divine, birth and death; *Hades*, of corruption and generation; *Scylla and Charybdis*, of nature and art; the *Cyclops*, of love and life (in theory); *Circe*, of love and life (in practice); and *Penelope*, of art and nature, of the human (as opposed to the divine) trinity, of sexual and other forms of love.

Three Propositions

It may be seen that the chapters move towards three final propositions. The first is that (I) *art frees from denial (Telemachus), from ethereality (Calypso), from pomposity (Aeolus), from authoritarianism (Wandering Rocks), from illusion (Nausicaa), and from deception (Eumaeus).*

The second proposition holds that (II) *art affirms the present as against the past and future (Nestor), the human as against the divine and sub-human (Lotus-Eaters), sensitivity as against callousness and airiness (Lestrygonians), actuality as against trumpery indignation or sentimentality (Sirens), natural processes as against unnatural and supernatural ones (Oxen of the Sun), sympathy as against detachment and statistical prying (Ithaca).*

According to the third proposition, (III) *love – the mainspring of art as of life – makes possible the joining of first and last things (Proteus), of death and birth (Hades), of nature and art (Scylla and Charybdis), of real and ideal (Cyclops), of body and soul (Circe), of art and nature (Penelope).*

Having completed his plan, Joyce might well feel that he had succeeded in disengaging what was affirmable in existence, and had affirmed that.

Appendix

The Linati and Gorman–Gilbert Schemas Compared

The first known schema for *Ulysses* was that which on 21 September 1920 Joyce sent to Carlo Linati. In the accompanying letter, he said, 'in view of the enormous bulk and the more than enormous complexity of my damned monster-novel it would be better to send . . . a sort of summary-key-skeleton-schema (for home use only). . . . I have given only ''Schlagworte'' [catchwords] in my schema but I think you will understand it all the same. It is the epic of two races (Israel-Ireland) and at the same time the cycle of the human body as well as a little story of a day (life). . . . It is also a kind of encyclopedia.'

The schema sent to Linati offers brief meanings (*Senso, Significato*) for each episode, lists the classical or legendary personages (some unexpected) without specifying their parallels, and names the several dominant symbols in each chapter. Joyce subsequently retracted some of his hints, especially of the episodes' meanings, and spelled out the less central classical parallels. He then devised a new schema, which in late 1921 he lent to Valery Larbaud, who was about to lecture on the still unpublished book.

After its publication, Joyce discreetly continued to circulate this second schema, or one like it, usually through Sylvia Beach's intermediary hands. Through her it reached Herbert

Gorman, Edmund Wilson, and others. Each of them was honour-bound not to make it public. At last, in Stuart Gilbert's *James Joyce's 'Ulysses'*, Joyce authorized its publication, but evidently specified that the classical-modern parallels should be set out in Gilbert's exegesis rather than as part of the author's plan. The second schema was not published complete until H. K. Croessmann edited it for the *James Joyce Miscellany* (Second Series, 1960). He used the plan Joyce had sent to Herbert Gorman, but it was virtually identical with the one Gilbert had had.

In the following charts, the Linati schema is given in the Italian original* and then in translation. At the right of the translated version are given (1) a table of correspondences which appears only in the Gorman plan, and (2) a list of variants between the Gorman–Gilbert plan on the one hand and the Linati schema on the other.

* Reproduced here, by permission of The Society of Authors and the Administrators of the Estate of James Joyce, from a copy of the manuscript kindly furnished by the Poetry Room of the University Library, State University of New York at Buffalo. A photograph of the manuscript appears on the front and back endpapers.

	Titolo	Ora	Colore	Persone	Tecnica	Scienza, Arte	Senso (Significat
					I. ALBA		
1	Telemachus	8–9	oro, bianco	Telemaco Antinoo ⎰ Mentor ⎱ Pallas I Proci Penelope (Musa)	Dialogo a 3 & 4 Narrazione Soliloquio	Teologia	Il figlio sp destato lotta
2	Nestore	9–10	marrone	Nestore Telemaco Pisistrato Elena	Dialogo a 2 Narrazione Soliloquio	Storia	La savieza vecchio
3	Proteo	10–11	azzurro	Proteo Menelao Elena Megapente Telemaco	Soliloquio	Filologia	La Prima materia (ΠΡΟ
					II. MATTINA		
1(4)	Calypso	8–9	arancio	Calypso (Penelope 'moglie') Ulisse Callidike	Dialogo a 2 Soliloquio	Mitologia	Il viandar che par

	Title	Time	Colour	Persons	Technic	Science, Art	Sense (Meani
					I. DAWN		
1	Telemachus	8–9	Gold White	Telemachus Antinoos ⎰ Mentor ⎱ Pallas The Suitors Penelope (Muse)	3- and 4-person dialogue Narration Soliloquy	Theology	The di posse son in strugg
2	Nestor	9–10	Chestnut	Nestor Telemachus Pisistratus Helen	2-person dialogue Narration Soliloquy	History	The w of the world
3	Proteus	10–11	Blue	Proteus Menelaus Helen Megapenthes Telemachus	Soliloquy	Philology	Prima mater (ΠΡΟ
					II. MORNING		
1(4)	Calypso	8–9	Orange	Calypso (Penelope 'wife') Ulysses Callidike	2-person dialogue Soliloquy	Mythology	The de ing tr ler

—	Amleto, Irlanda, Stefano
(Telemaco non soffre ancora il corpo)	
	Ulster, Donna, Senso Pratico
	Parola, Marca, **Luna,** Evoluzione, Metamorfosi
·eni	Vagina, Esiglio, Famiglia, Nimfa, Israele in Schiavitù

GORMAN–GILBERT PLAN

·ɔ	Symbol	Correspondences	Variants from Linati schema
	Hamlet, Ireland, Stephen	Stephen- Telemachus – Hamlet: Buck Mulligan – Antinoos: Milkwoman – Mentor	Scene: The Tower Hour: 8 a.m. Symbol: Heir Technic: Narrative (young)
(Telemachus does not yet bear a body)	Ulster, Woman, Common Sense	Deasy – Nestor: Pisistratus – Sargent: Helen – Mrs O'Shea	Scene: The School Hour: 10 a.m. Colour: Brown Symbol: Horse Technic: Catechism (personal)
	Word, Signature, Moon, Evolution, Metamorphosis	Proteus–Primal Matter: Kevin Egan–Menelaus: Magapenthes – The Cocklepickers	Scene: The Strand Hour: 11 a.m. Colour: Green Symbol: Tide Technic: Monologue (male)
·ieys	Vagina, Exile, Family, Nymph, Israel in bondage	Calypso – The Nymph, Dlugacz: The Recall : Zion – Ithaca	Scene: The House Hour: 8 a.m. Art: Economics Symbol: Nymph Technic: Narrative (mature)

Titolo	Ora	Colore	Persone	Tecnica	Scienza, Arte	Senso (Significato)
			(II. MATTINA)			
2(5) Lotofaghi	9–10	bruno	Eurilocho Polite Ulisse Nausikaa(2)	Dialogo Soliloquio Preghiera	Chimica	La Seduzion della Fede
3(6) Hades	11–12	nero-bianco	Ulisse Elpenor Ajace Agamemnone Ercole Eriphyle Sisifo Orione Laerte ecc Prometeo Cerbero Tiresia Hades Proserpina Telemaco Antinoo	Narrazione Dialoghi		Discesa nel Nulla

Title	Time	Colour	Persons	Technic	Science, Art	Sense (Meaning)
			(II. MORNING)			
2(5) Lotus-Eaters	9–10	Brown	Eurylochus Polites Ulysses Nausicaa(2)	Dialogue Soliloquy Prayer	Chemistry	The Seduction of the Faith
3(6) Hades	11–12	Black White	Ulysses Elpenor Ajax Agamemnon Hercules Eriphyle Sisyphus Orion Laertes etc. Prometheus Cerberus Tiresias Hades Proserpina Telemachus Antinoos	Narration Dialogues	--	Descent to Nothing

Ostia, Pene nel
bagno, Schiuma,
Fiore: Droghe:
Castrazione: Avena
Cimitero: Sacro
Cuore: Il Passato:
L'ignoto: L'Incon-
scio: Vizio Cardi-
aco: Reliquie:
Crepacuore

Symbol	Correspondences	Variants from Linati schema
Host, Penis in Bath, Foam, Flower: Drugs: Castration: Oats	Lotus-eaters – Cab-horses, Communicants, Soldiers, Eunuchs, Bather, Watchers of Cricket	Scene: The Bath Hour: 10 a.m. Organ: Genitals Art: Botany, chemistry Colour: None Symbol: Eucharist Technic: Narcissism
Cemetery: Sacred Heart: The Past: The Unknown Man· The Unconscious: Heart trouble: Relics: Heartbreak	Dodder, Grand and Royal Canals, Liffey – The 4 Rivers: Cunningham – Sisyphus: Father Coffey – Cerberus: Caretaker – Hades: Daniel O'Connell – Hercules: Dignam – Elpenor: Parnell – Agamemnon Menton – Ajax	Scene: The Graveyard Hour: 11 a.m. Art: Religion Symbol: Caretaker Technic: Incubism

	Titolo	Ora	Colore	Persone	Tecnica	Scienza, Arte	Senso (Significato)
				MEZZOGIORNO			
4(7)	Eolo	12–1	rosso	Eolo Figli Telemaco Mentore Ulisse(2)	Simboleutike Dikanike Epidiktike Tropi	Rettorica	L'Irrisione della Vitt01
5(8)	Lestrigoni	1–2	sanguigno	Antifate La Figlia Allettatrice Ulisse	Prosa peristaltica	Archittetura	L'Abattimer
6(9)	Scylla e Caridde	2–3	—	Scylla e Caridde Ulisse Telemaco Antinoo	Gorghi	Letteratura	Dilemma Bitagliente

	Title	Time	Colour	Persons	Technic	Science, Art	Sense (Meaning)
				NOON			
4(7)	*Aeolus*	12–1	Red	Aeolus Sons Telemachus Mentor Ulysses(2)	Simbouleutike [deliberative oratory] Dikanike [forensic oratory] Epideictic [public oratory] Tropes	Rhetoric	The Mockery of Victory
5(8)	*Lestry-gonians*	1–2	Blood colour	Antiphates The seductive daughter Ulysses	Peristaltic prose	Architecture	Dejection
6(9)	*Scylla and Charybdis*	2–3	—	Scylla and Charybdis Ulysses Telemachus Antinoos	Whirlpools	Literature	Two-edged dilemma

gano	Simbolo
oni	Maschine: Vento: Fame: Cervo vol- ante: Destini Mancati: Stampa: mutabilità
go	Sacrifizio cruento: cibi: vergogna
ello	Amleto, Shakespeare, Cristo, Socrate, Londra e Stratford, Scolasticismo e Mis- ticismo, Platone e Aristotele, Gio- ventà e Maturità

n	Symbol	Correspondences	Variants from Linati schema
	Machine: Wind: Hunger: Stag Beetle: Failed Destinies: Press: Mutability	Crawford – Aeolus: Incest – Journalism: Floating Island – Press	Scene: The Newspaper Hour: 12 noon Symbol: Editor Technic: Enthymemic
agus	Bloody sacrifice: foods: shame	Antiphates – Hunger: The Decoy: Food: Lestrygonians – Teeth	Scene: The Lunch Hour: 1 p.m. Colour: None Symbol: Constables
	Hamlet, Shakespeare, Christ, Socrates, London and Stratford, Scholasticism and Mysticism, Plato and Aristotle, Youth and Maturity	The Rock – Aristotle, Dogma, Stratford: The Whirlpool – Plato, Mysticism, London: Ulysses – Socrates, Jesus, Shakespeare	Scene: The Library Hour: 2 p.m. Symbol: Stratford – London Technic: Dialectic

	Titolo	Ora	Colore	Persone	Tecnica	Scienza, Arte	Senso (Significato)
					GIORNO Finito Antiali-Ombelico		
7(10)	Roccie Erranti	3–4	arcobaleno	Oggetti Luoghi Forze Ulisse	Laberinto mobile fra due sponde	Meccanica	L'Ambiente Nemico
8(11)	Sirene	4–5	corallo	Leucotea Partenope Ulisse Orfeo Menelao Argonauti	Fuga per canonem	Musica	Il Dolce Inganno
9(12)	Ciclope	5–6	verde	Prometeo Nessuno (Io) Ulisse Galatea	Asimetria alternata	Chirurgia	Il Terrore Egocida

	Title	Time	Colour	Persons	Technic	Science, Art	Sense (Meaning)
					DAY (Anti-wings, umbilicus finished)		
7(10)	Wandering Rocks	3–4	Rainbow	Objects Places Forces Ulysses	Labyrinth moving between two banks	Mechanics	The Hostile Environment
8(11)	Sirens	4–5	Coral	Leucothea Parthenope Ulysses Orpheus Menelaus The Argonauts	Fuga per Canonem	Music	The Sweet Cheat
9(12)	Cyclops	5–6	Green	Prometheus No one (I) Ulysses Galatea	Alternating asymmetry	Surgery	The Ego-cidal Terror

	Simbolo
:e	Cristo e Cesare: Errori: Omonimi: Sincronismi: Rassomiglianze
:hio	Promesse: Feminismo: Suoni: Abellimenti
uscoli ssa	Nazione: Stato: Religione: Dinastia: Idealismo: Esagerazione: Fanatismo: Collettività

n	Symbol	Correspondences	Variants from Linati schema
	Christ and Caesar: Errors: Homonyms: Synchronizations: Resemblances	Bosporus – Liffey: European Bank – Viceroy: Asiatic Bank – Conmee: Symplegades – Groups of Citizens	Scene: The Streets Hour: 3 p.m. Colour: None Symbol: Citizens Technic: Labyrinth
	Promises: Feminism: Sounds: Embellishments	Sirens – Barmaids: Isle – bar	Scene: The Concert Room Hour: 4 p.m. Colour: None Symbol: Barmaids
Muscles Bones	Nation: State: Religion: Dynasty: Idealism: Exaggeration: Fanaticism: Collectivity	Noman – I: Stake – cigar: Challenge – apotheosis	Scene: The Tavern Hour: 5 p.m. Organ: Muscle Art: Politics Symbol: Fenian Technic: Gigantism

Titolo	Ora	Colore	Persone	Tecnica	Scienza, Arte	Senso (Significato)
				(GIORNO)		
10(13) Nausikaa	8–9	grigio	Nausikaa Ancelle Alcinoos Arete Ulisse	Progressione retrogressiva	Pittura	Il Miraggio Proiettato
11(14) Armenti del Sole	10–11	bianco	Lampetie Phaetusa Elio Iperione Giove Ulisse	Prosa (Embrione-Feto-Parto)	Fisica	Le Mandrie Eterne
12(15) Circe	11–12	viola	Circe Le Bestie Telemaco Ulisse Ermete	Visione animata fino allo scoppio	Danza	L'Orca Antropofol

Title	Time	Colour	Persons	Technic	Science, Art	Sense (Meaning)
				(DAY)		
10(13) Nausicaa	8–9	Grey	Nausicaa Handmaidens Alcinoos Arete Ulysses	Retrogressive progression	Painting	The Projected Mirage
11(14) Oxen of the Sun	10–11	White	Lampetie Phaethusa Helios Hyperion Jove Ulysses	Prose (Embryo-Foetus-Birth)	Physic	The Eternal Flocks
12(15) Circe	11–12	Violet	Circe The Beasts Telemachus Ulysses Hermes	Vision animated to bursting-point	Dance	The Man-Hating Orc

Organo	Simbolo
...io	Onanismo: Muliebre: Ipocrisia
...ice ...o	Fecondazione, frodi, parthenogenesi
...rato ...motore ...etro	Zoologia: personificazione: panteismo: magia: veleno: contraveleno: ridda

Organ	Symbol	Correspondences	Variants from Linati schema
	Onanism: Female: Hypocrisy	Phaeacia – Star of the Sea: Gerty – Nausicaa	Scene: The Rocks Hour: 8 p.m. Colour: Grey, blue Symbol: Virgin Technic: Tumescence, detumescence
...k ...s	Fecundation, frauds, parthenogenesis	Hospital – Trinacria: Lampetie, Phaethusa – Nurses: Helios – Horne: Oxen – Fertility: Crime – Fraud	Scene: The Hospital Hour: 10 p.m. Organ: Womb Art: Medicine Symbol: Mothers Technic: Embryonic development
...iotor ...ratus ...on	Zoology: personification: pantheism: magic: poison: antidote: reel	Circe – Bella	Scene: The Brothel Hour: 12 midnight Art: Magic Colour: None Symbol: Whore Technic: Hallucination

	Titolo	Ora	Colore	Persone	Tecnica	Scienza, Arte	Senso (Significato)
				III. *MEZZANOTTE* (Fusione di Bloom e Stephen) (Ulis. e Tel.)			
1(16)	Eumeo	12–1	—	Eumeo Ulisse Telemaco Il Cattivo Pastore Ulisse Pseudangelo	Prosa rilassata		L'Imboscat Indigena
2(17)	Ithaca	1–2	— stellare lattea	Ulisse Telemaco Eurycleia I Proci	Dialogo Stile pacato Fusione		La Speranz Armata
3(18)	Penelope	∞	stellare lattea *poi* nuova alba	Laerte Ulisse Penelope	Monologo Stile rassegnato		Il Passato Dorme

NOTTE ALTA — *ALBA*

↓ ↓

Ulisse (Bloom) Telemaco (Stephen)

	Title	Time	Colour	Persons	Technic	Science, Art	Sense (Meaning)
				III. *MIDNIGHT* (Fusion of Bloom and Stephen) (Ulysses and Telemachus)			
1(16)	*Eumaeus*	12–1	—	Eumaeus Ulysses Telemachus The Bad Shepherd Ulysses Pseudangelos	Relaxed prose		The Ambush at Home
2(17)	*Ithaca*	1–2	— starry milky	Ulysses Telemachus Eurycleia The Suitors	Dialogue Pacified style Fusion		The Armed Hope
3(18)	*Penelope*	∞	starry milky *then* new dawn	Laertes Ulysses Penelope	Monologue Resigned style		The Past Sleeps

DEEP NIGHT — *DAWN*

↓ ↓

Ulysses (Bloom) Telemachus (Step

Organo	Simbolo
Nervi	
Succhi	
Grasso	

gan	Symbol	Correspondences	Variants from Linati schema
Nerves		Eumaeus – Skin the Goat: Sailor – Ulysses Pseudangelos: Melanthius – Corley	Scene: The Shelter Hour: 1 a.m. Art: Navigation Symbol: Sailors Technic: Narrative (old)
Juices		Eurymachus – Boylan: Suitors – scruples: Bow – reason	Scene: The House Hour: 2 a.m. Organ: Skeleton Art: Science Symbol: Comets Technic: Catechism (impersonal)
Fat		Penelope – Earth: Web – Movement	Scene: The Bed Hour: None Symbol: Earth Technic: Monologue (female)

Notes

A few details in the Preface to this book are borrowed from my essay, '*Ulysses*: A Short History', which is appended to the Penguin edition of *Ulysses* (London, 1969). Quotations from Joyce's letters are from the three-volume edition, *Letters of James Joyce* (New York and London, 1966), unless otherwise indicated.

p. 1
unfixed in June 1915   Joyce's postcard to Stanislaus Joyce of this date is included in my edition of the *Selected Letters of James Joyce*, now in the press.

p. 2
favourite number as well   See Cedric H. Whitman, *Homer and the Heroic Tradition* (Cambridge, Mass., 1958), p. 256.

p. 3
(Svevo's grandfather was Hungarian.) It seems probable now that Svevo rather than Teodoro Meyer (as suggested in my biography of Joyce) was a principal model for Bloom. Svevo's grandfather was from Kopcen, Hungary. See P. N. Furbank, *Italo Svevo* (London, 1966), p. 3.

p. 5
'. . . *whose son he was*'   *The Story of Odysseus*, trans. W. H. D. Rouse (New York, n.d.), p. 6.

p. 9
enmattered its essence   Aristotle, *De Anima* (402), in *The Basic Works of Aristotle*, ed. Richard McKeon (New York, 1968), p. 537.

p. 17
The law of contradiction   Aristotle, *Metaphysics* (1006), ibid., pp. 737–8.

Stephen declares   'Aristotle's entire system of philosophy rests upon his book of psychology and that, I think, rests on his statement that the same attribute cannot at the same time and in the same connection belong to and not belong to the same subject.' *A Portrait of the Artist as a Young Man* (New York, 1964), p. 208.

incorporeal things   Aristotle, *Metaphysics* (988), *Basic Works*, p. 703.

the form of forms   Aristotle, *De Anima* (431–2), ibid., p. 595.

p. 29
'*Who is good?*'   'James Clarence Mangan', *The Critical Writings of James Joyce* (New York and London, 1957), p. 76.

p. 30
'. . . *armed warriors*'   Frank Budgen, *James Joyce and the Making of 'Ulysses'* (1934, reissued Bloomington, Ind., 1960), pp. 15–17, and interview with Budgen.

p. 50
'. . . *kingdom of the dead*'   *The Story of Odysseus*, p. 139.

p. 52
'. . . *experience comprehended*'   A. Robert Caponigri, *Time and Idea, the Theory of History in Giambattista Vico* (London, 1953), p. 133.

p. 54
the least cold   Giordano Bruno, *Cause, Principle, and Unity*, trans. Jack Lindsay (London, 1962), p. 148.

love is hate, hate love   J. Lewis McIntyre, *Giordano Bruno* (London, 1903), p. 164.

p. 55
'. . . *and generation?*'   Bruno, *Cause, Principle, and Unity*, p. 149.

p. 56
'. . . *and of all forms*'   Giordano Bruno, *De la Causa, principio et uno*, quoted in Dorothea Waley Singer, *Giordano Bruno* (New York, 1950), p. 100.

'. . . *truth and good*'   Ibid., p. 101.

as in a seed   Ibid.

p. 79
'*imagination was memory*'   Frank Budgen, *Myselves When Young* (London, 1970), p. 187.

p. 80

his Gorgonzola sandwich   This cheese is probably chosen because of Dante's adventure with the Gorgon in the *Inferno*, IX. Bloom masters the monster by digesting her. Cf. S. L. Goldberg, *The Classical Temper* (London, 1961), p. 129.

p. 82

his business acumen.   See S. Schoenbaum, *Shakespeare's Lives* (Oxford and New York, 1970), pp. 645–57.

p. 95

'. . . *as philosophical difficulties*'   David Hume, *A Treatise of Human Nature*, ed. L. A. Selby-Bigge (Oxford, 1928), p. 262.

'. . . *reasonings and speculations*'   Ibid., p. 187.

less ultimate than Aristotle's   For a comment on these contradictions, see John Passmore, *Hume's Intentions* (London, 1968), p. 143.

'. . . *idea of extension*'   Hume, *Treatise*, p. 33.

p. 96

'. . . *by the mind*'   Ibid., p. 35.

'. . . *idea of time*'   Ibid., p. 36.

tentative the better   Stuart Gilbert declares that the 'spirit of incertitude is materialized in the *Circe* episode. . . .' *James Joyce's 'Ulysses'* (1934; reissued New York, 1952), p. 222.

'. . . *or common life*'   Hume, *Treatise*, p. 185.

'. . . *all these chimeras*'   Ibid., p. 269.

'. . . *any farther*'   Ibid.

'. . . *his philosophical conviction*'   Ibid., p. 273.

'. . . *arguments in time*'   Ibid., p. 187.

p. 104

through all its tricks   Yeats spoke of music as the 'deadly foe' of literary art. See 'The Evils of Too Much Print', *Literary Digest* (11 March 1911), p. 461. Quoted in Lawrance Thompson, *Robert Frost: The Early Years 1874–1915* (New York, 1966), p. 376.

p. 109

'. . . *the bridge sky-high*'   Stuart Gilbert, *James Joyce's 'Ulysses'*, p. 28. Gilbert puts the statement in the third person but says *ipse dixit*.

p. 115

poets in English   Joyce did not admit to liking *Prometheus Unbound*, and spoke of it quite curtly to Frank Budgen. But he used it notwithstanding, close to the core of his own work.

towards eternity now   Joyce had earlier, in *Stephen Hero*, given Christ a mock-apotheosis. Stephen asks his mother 'do you mean to tell me you believe that our friend went up off the mountain as they say he did?' Over her protests he goes on, 'He comes into the world God knows how, walks on the water, gets out of his grave and goes up off the Hill of Howth.' *Stephen Hero* (New York, 1963), p. 133.

p. 129

'. . . *artist about old Bloom*'   Cf. Anna Livia on Earwicker, 'But there is a great poet in you too.' *Finnegans Wake* (New York and London, 1939), p. 619.

p. 142

'. . . *and true knowledge*'   The passage continues, 'Here is a real world, and of this world man is truly the God.' Benedetto Croce, *The Philosophy of Giambattista Vico*, trans. R. G. Collingwood (1913; reissued London, 1964), p. 29.

p. 145

the name 'Noman'   Another play on sounds, as Nathan Halper has reminded me, is that of 'Agendath' (usually transliterated 'Agudoth') and 'Agenbite'.

p. 148

decision was for Yeats   Joyce may have remembered that in 'The Autumn of the Body', an important early essay, Yeats predicted that a new work on Ulysses might be written.

p. 154

crossed the Equator   I owe this suggestion to Mary Reynolds.

p. 155

as Gilbert points out   Gilbert, *James Joyce's 'Ulysses'*, p. 351.

p. 161

are always men   Mary Ellmann, in *Thinking About Women* (New York and London, 1968).

p. 162

mouth at last   Joyce probably regarded S as a male letter (Gerty MacDowell relates Bloom to a snake staring at its prey), and Y as a female one. (He said in a letter that 'yes' was a female word.) For this literal symbolism he had precedents in Mallarmé and Rimbaud, not to mention Dante. It may be noted here that he draws another circle by making the *Telemachiad* begin with S and end with P, and the *Nostos* begin with P and end with S.

Compare *Stephen Hero*, p. 32 : '. . . he put his lines together not word by word but letter by letter. He read Blake and Rimbaud on the values of letters and even permuted and combined the five vowels to construct cries for primitive emotions.'

p. 173

that nature makes   The whole passage in *The Winter's Tale*, IV. iv, 86–97, is relevant:

Perdita: For I have heard it said
   There is an art which, in their piedness, shares
   With great creating nature.
Polixenes: Say there be;
   Yet nature is made better by no mean,
   But nature makes that mean: so o'er that art
   Which you say adds to nature is an art
   That nature makes. You see, sweet maid, we marry
   A gentler scion to the wildest stock,
   And make conceive a bark of baser kind
   By bud of nobler race. This is an art
   Which mends nature, – changes it rather; but
   The art itself is nature.

In the same vein, Dante has Virgil explain in the *Inferno*, XI, that '*vostr'arte a Dio quasi è nipote*', that is, that God's child is nature whose child is art.

INDEX

Detailed discussion of an entry is indicated by bold face.

7 [6] Rocce Erranti : 3-4 : arcobaleno : Oggetti : Labirinto
Luoghi fra due spr
Ulisse

8 [11] Sirene : 4-5 : corallo : Leucotea : Fuga per
Partenope Canone
Ulisse
Orfeo
Blindes
Argonauti

9 [12] Ciclope : 5-6 : verde : Prometeo : Asimetria
Nessuno (Io) alternata
Ulisse
Galatea

10 [9] Nausicaa : 8-9 : grigio : Nausicaa : Progressione
ancelle Retrogressione
Alcinoo
Arete
Ulisse

11 [18] Armenti del Sole : 10-11 : bianco : Lampetie : Feto / Embrio
Phaethusa - Feto - Par
Elio Iperione
Giove
Ulisse

12 [15] Circe : 11-12 : viola : Circe : Visione
Le Bestie Animata
Telemaco fino allo
Ulisse scoppio
Ermete

1 [16] Eumeo : 12-1 : ∧ : Eumeo : Prova
Ulisse Ridomata
Telemaco
Il falso padre
Ulisse falso figlio

2 [17] Itaca : 1-2 : ∖ : Ulisse : Dialogo
stelle Telemaco Stile Placca
lattea Eumeo Fusione
I Rivali

3 [18] Penelope : ∞ : stelle : Laerte : Monologo
lattea Ulisse Stile Lassitudine
noi nuova alba Penelope

Notte

Ulisse / B